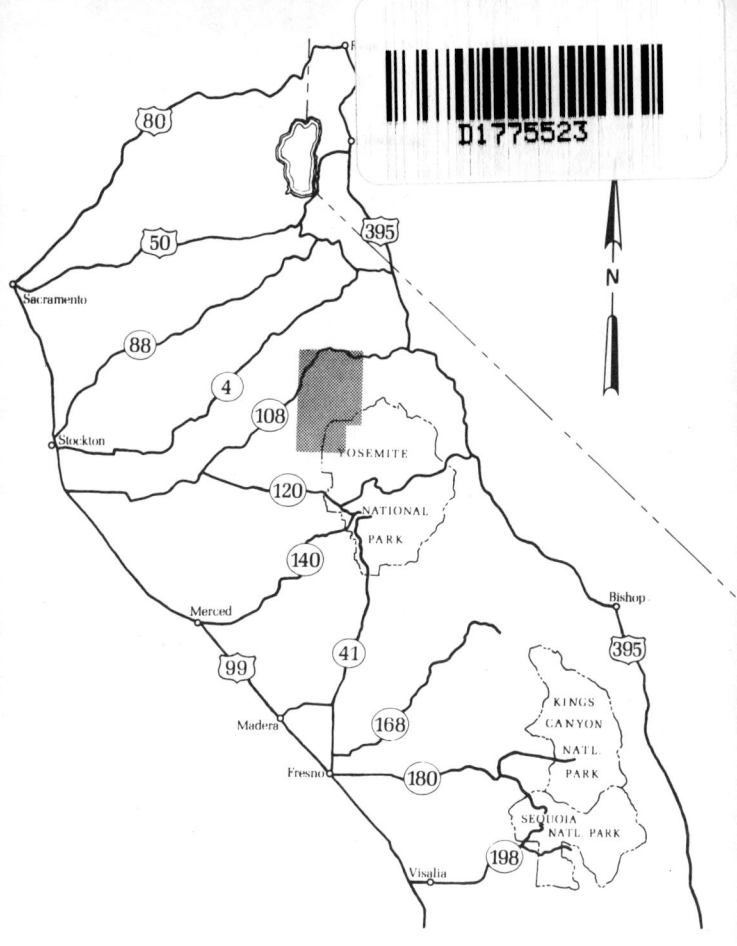

Location of the area covered by this guide

High Sierra Hiking Guide #19

Pinecrest

by Ben Schifrin

Photos by the author
except as indicated

Wilderness Press

BERKELEY

Copyright © 1976 by Wilderness Press

Library of Congress Card Number 75-38173

SBN: 911824-48-0

Manufactured in the United States

Introduction

THE HIGH SIERRA HIKING GUIDES by the editors of Wilderness Press and other outdoor writers are the first *complete* guides to the famous High Sierra. Each guide covers one 15-minute U.S.G.S. topographic quadrangle, which is an area about 14 miles east-west by 17 miles north-south. The first page shows the location of the area covered by this guide.

There is a great and increasing demand for literature about America's favorite wilderness, John Muir's "Range of Light." To meet this demand, we have undertaken this guide series. The purpose of each book in the series is threefold: first, to provide a reliable basis for planning a trip, second, to serve as a field guide while you are on the trail; and third, to stimulate you to further field investigation and background reading. In each guide, there are a minimum of 100 described miles of trails, and the descriptions are supplemented with maps and other logistical and background information. HIGH SIERRA HIKING GUIDES are based on first-hand observation. There is absolutely no substitute for walking the trails, so we walked all the trails.

In planning this series, we chose the 15-minute quadrangle as the unit because — though every way of dividing the Sierra is arbitrary — the topographic quadrangle map ("topo map") is the chosen aid of almost every wilderness traveler. Inside the back cover of this book is a large map of all the area the book covers, showing described trails and cross-country routes. With this map, you can always get where you want to go, with a minimum of detours or wasted effort.

One other thing the wilderness traveler will need: a wilderness permit from the Forest Service. A permit is required for an overnight stay or even a day visit to the Emigrant Wilderness. You can obtain your permit by mail or in person at the ranger stations listed below.

Summit District Ranger Station (for west-side entry)
Box 1295
Pinecrest CA 95370 (at the Pinecrest "Y")

Groveland District Ranger Station (for south-side entry)
Groveland CA 95321 ("downtown")

Your Forest Service permit is also good if you cross over into Yosemite Park on foot.

Wilson Meadow Lake

Table of Contents

The Country . . . . page 1

The History 3

The Geology 9

The Ecosystem 17

The Trails 31

Trail Descriptions 33

Climbers 113

Bibliography 115

Index 117

Starvation Lake

The Country

THE WILDERNESS REgion lying east of Pinecrest Lake and north of Cherry Reservoir is a hospitable land, yet one of startling contrasts that afford attractions for all, from families with small children to technical rock climbers. The *Pinecrest* quadrangle sits astride the boundary between the rolling volcanic ridges and quiet forests of the northern Sierra, little-visited by outdoor enthusiasts, and the better-known, often overcrowded High Sierra to the south, with its alpine grandeur, craggy precipices, and granitic barrenness. This juxtaposition of dissimilarities has created in *Pinecrest* a diversity of terrains and attractions for all.

In the northern one third of the *Pinecrest* quadrangle, cobbly volcanic soil supports thick forests of lodgepole pines amid spiry parapets such as East Flange Rock and the Three Chimneys, while the lower two thirds is composed of typical Sierran granite, only sparingly clad in conifers. But this Yosemite-like granitic country is subtly different from that farther south. Here, Ice Age glaciers bit deep into the bedrock, sculpting curvaceous domes and gouging sheer-walled chasms instead of the frail cockscombs and Matterhorned peaks which characterize much of the Sierra farther south. Instead of a steepled landscape, glaciers here left row upon row of smooth ridges interspersed with sparkling water, either in the form of meandering rivers looping through lazy backwaters in verdant meadows, glimmering lakes strung like sapphire necklaces, or as tumultuous cataracts plunging wildly through twisting gorges. These ridges and their attendant valleys allow easy access to almost any point in *Pinecrest*, while water, in its many moods, provides much of the Emigrant Basin's attraction. Fighting trout inhabit most any pool or lake and draw thousands of anglers every season. Nonfishermen can relax on the banks of lake or stream, soaking up the sun which is only rarely displaced by summer thundershowers, and enjoy nosegays of fragrant subalpine blossoms while their toes wriggle in a tussock of brilliant emerald grasses, if they find the right spot!

This hospitable land is available to almost anyone most of the year. Pinecrest Lake and Cherry Reservoir are usually snow-free by early May, and even the highest elevations are accessible late in June. The high country then stays open well into October, when a nip returns to the air, quaking aspens turn valley bottoms into conflagrations of blazing yellow, and rainbow trout erupt in frenzied feeding. Even in winter, when deep snows settle in a mysterious white blanket, properly equipped cross-country ski-tourers can easily penetrate to the Emigrant Wilderness' heart to discover the silent season in *Pinecrest*.

In summer, when *Pinecrest* receives the most traffic, there is room for all and trips to suit any taste and any group. Well-maintained trails crisscross the region, making possible day hikes or week-long jaunts suitable for young or old. Most trips involve relatively little elevation gain, but the ambitious naturalist can nevertheless find four different "life zones" within *Pinecrest*'s confines. The lower country in the west is decked in restful forests of mixed conifers, home for a multitude of wildlife and temporary haven for human campers. At *Pinecrest*'s highest point, 10,322' Granite Dome, one stands above timberline, gazing south to the Minarets and north to the ruddy mountains rimming Lake Tahoe, with naught but blue sky and maybe a red-tailed hawk wheeling overhead.

For the adventuresome and energetic, *Pinecrest* also has its pleasures. Many remote tarns and meadowed valleys are not reached by trails, but this glaciated country is so open that cross-country travel in it is almost unrestricted. Untrod cross-country routes provide freedom from designated trails, and lead to virginal campsites in snug hemlock bowers.

Finally, unbeknownst to most, *Pinecrest* is a rock climber's delight. High, clean walls that soar from almost every canyon provide fine backcountry climbing without the queues or crud of more popularized cliffs.

There is room for all in the gentle embrace of *Pinecrest*'s hills and hollows. Find your niche, lie back, relax, and leave behind the trifling worries of the weekday world.

The History

THE MIWOK INDIANS were the first men to visit the pristine upper reaches of the Stanislaus and Tuolumne rivers, but they never lingered long. Captain Gabriel Moraga, leading a Spanish expedition to establish inland missions, was the first European to see the Stanislaus, which he named "Rio de Nuestra Senora de Guadalupe." The Stanislaus received its present name after 1827, when a Miwok, forced by the Spaniards to work in peonage at Mission San Jose, ran away and fomented a general uprising among his relatives in the Central Valley. Named Stanislas by the missionaries, he and his followers battled the Spanish on the river that now bears his name.

Most of the Miwoks in the region around *Pinecrest* lived in the Upper Sonoran life zone, which is the biotic community of the Sierra foothills up to almost 4000 feet. Because they couldn't store enough food to last the winter months in higher elevations, the Miwoks were not able to live permanently in the higher biotic communities that compose most of the hiking country in *Pinecrest*. But Miwoks did venture into the High Sierra, especially in summer and fall, when their lower homes became hot, and acorns were ripe and hunting prosperous in the upper climes. In the summer, too, the Miwoks traded with their eastern neighbors, the Piutes, for obsidian, giving acorns and other food in return.

Like other California natives, the Miwoks had relatively mild living conditions, but even so they had to work every day. Most of their time was spent in the laborious gathering of grain staples. The nuts of Digger pines were one dietary mainstay. A foothill tree, its name is rooted in the white man's epithet "Digger" for the Miwoks, who spent much time foraging for bulbs of mariposa lilies and brodaiea. In late summer they harvested the nuts of Transition Zone sugar pines, and in the fall they collected black-oak acorns, a major staple, and manzanita berries.

The Miwoks also hunted in *Pinecrest*, stalking mule deer, snaring ground squirrels and netting fish. It is interesting to note that the Indians, like most game, traveled on ridges, avoiding the clammy, brush-choked canyons in which white men usually build their trails.

The decline and fall of the Miwok culture was swift. Except for a few incursions by Spanish missionaries, the Sierra Miwoks had little to do with Europeans until a man named Woods found gold in the stream near Jamestown that now bears his name. The great Gold Rush of 1849 sent droves of miners into the heart of the Miwoks' domain. The 49ers, bringing with them callousness, greed, racism and disease, quickly eliminated the Miwoks.

The Gold Rush brought an upsurge of interest in the *Pinecrest* area. Gold was the reason for this period of exploration. People entering the high country were either looking for it, traveling over the Sierra to reach the places it was found, or building dams to allow hydraulic mining downstream.

The first emigrants to cross the Sierra near *Pinecrest* were the Bartleson-Bidwell Party of 1841, well before the discovery of gold. California had other attractions, and in 1841 their wagon train left Missouri bound for this promised land. On October 18, having been forced to leave their wagons behind, they crossed the Sierra crest in the vicinity of Emigrant Pass (in *Tower Peak* quadrangle). With great difficulty, the Bartleson-Bidwell marched west through the northern reaches of *Pinecrest* country, and finally reached the Great Valley, but not before young Bidwell had stumbled upon the South Grove of Calaveras Big Trees, the first sighting of these giant sequoias.

The next group of pioneers to attempt the Sonora route was the Clark-Skidmore Party in 1852. This group of men, 75 strong, managed to get their wagons far up the eastern slope of the Sierra, but an early snowstorm engulfed them and forced them to abandon the wagons. Able to push on only a bit farther, they descended to a sheltered spot in a small valley. A few men kept going, reached a ranch near Soulsbyville, and brought back a rescue party. Their bivouac site was in what we call Lower Relief Valley.

By the next year, 1853, Sonora was a growing boom town. The citizens, desirous of community growth and commerce, sent Mayor George Washington Patrick to Humbolt, Nevada, the staging ground for trans-Sierra emigrant trains, to try to tap some of that never-ending human stream for the Sonora Trail. Possessed of a glib and artful tongue, the good mayor proceeded to regale travelers with the virtues of Emigrant Pass and the deathly dangers of all other passes. He found takers in the combined Duckwall and Trahern parties. The Duckwall group had only 11 members, but the party of Cherokee Indians led by George Washington Trahern was much larger. They brought with them 500 head of cattle. To surmount Emigrant Pass, these hardy pioneers had to construct their own grade, for only the most rudimentary path existed. Gorges had to be filled with rocks, trees felled, and steep bluffs ascended before the travelers emerged on the comparatively easy slopes around Emigrant Pass. But the worst was yet to come. Descending the valley of Summit Creek, their way was blocked by domes and precipices which threatened destruction of their wagons and worldly possessions. By hitching some oxen behind their wagons to hold them back, the Duckwall Party finally negotiated this treacherous canyon to reach Upper Relief Valley on September 27, 1853. The Trahern Party, after losing two wagons on the steep descent, reached this grassland the following day. Once again snow fell prematurely, and the band had to send word to Sonora for help. Like previous parties, they then proceeded to Whitesides Meadow and generally along the volcanic-capped ridge just south of the South Fork Stanislaus River's headwaters, paralleling Main Trail #4 in this guide. Past Lake Valley, where a later group was stranded by snow, and Burst Rock (a corruption of "Birth Rock" — a pioneer baby was born in its shelter) the Duckwall-Trahern Party descended Dodge Ridge to Sonora.

Little was done to improve the Emigrant Pass route until gold was discovered in 1858 at Bodie, and a bit later at Aurora. There was a mass exodus toward these gold fields by way of much easier, more northern trails. The desire to compete with these routes spurred completion, by 1864, of a wagon road over Sonora Pass, some 8 miles north of Emigrant Pass.

During this time much mining was still going on in the region just west of *Pinecrest*, but the miners' main interest in the quadrangle was not so much in gold, which was rare in these upper reaches, but in the copious water, which was used to mine the gold flakes that had been washed from the high country and then deposited near Sonora and Columbia. These elusive specks of "color" were mixed with many feet of alluvium, so miners sprayed powerful streams of water on the soil, then allowed the heavier gold to settle in the bottoms of mesh sluices, where it was easily collected. By 1858, miners had built a series of flumes and ditches to Donnells Flat, now the site of Donnells Reservoir, to utilize the Middle Fork Stanislaus River as a water supply for hydraulic mines. At the same time, they dug a tunnel from the South Fork to the Middle Fork so that the former's waters might also be tapped. To ensure adequate flow year-round, they then built three storage reservoirs near the South Fork's headwaters. The lowest of these stood where Pinecrest Lake now lies. Just above it was a smaller lake called Eleanor Lake. Some 1800 feet higher, at 7350 feet, was the largest impoundment, called Gertrude Lake or Big Dam. The Big Dam was big. It was almost 450 feet long and held water to a depth of 62 feet, making it the largest all-wood dam in the world. All three dams were built by Chinese labor entirely of massive timbers cut on the site. Big Dam burned down in the '20s, but a few timbers can still be seen in the creek, and spikes driven into the rock nearby indicate its dimensions.

The dam at Eleanor Lake is in much better repair. Some stonework and one complete segment of the dam still remain, as indicated in Cross-Country Route #3. Scattered around in

The History

the general area one will find spikes and eyelets driven into the granite, and cable and rusted hulks of machinery. They are the remnants of steam donkeys, powerful steam-driven winches which could literally pull themselves up a mountain. These engines were used to haul and set timbers and boulders for the dams.

Since the 1860s men have been bringing cattle into the area now designated the Emigrant Wilderness, to fatten them on the rich subalpine grasses. A man named Cooper first ran cattle into the upper South Fork Stanislaus in the 1860s. Another, named Rosasco, ran cattle in Piute Meadow and built a cabin there around 1880. Later, a young Sonoran named Fred Leighton helped to herd cattle that grazed much of the *Pinecrest* wilderness from Piute Meadow to Long and Emigrant lakes. Leighton noticed that few fish could be found throughout the basin — most of the streams dried up soon after the snows melted because there was little soil to absorb the moisture. In 1916 Leighton built a cabin at Yellowhammer Lake and erected small rock-and-concrete dams at Yellowhammer, Leighton and Red Can lakes, so that water could be slowly released later in the season. These dams kept the streams below running year-round. In 1931 Leighton raised money to pay for five more dams, on Bigelow, Emigrant Meadow, Emigrant, Lower Buck and Long lakes, so that all of Cherry Creek would flow all summer, allowing trout to be planted in waters that had been barren. In all, 16 check dams have been constructed in the Emigrant Wilderness, and they ensure not only running water in the later part of summer, but excellent angling in more than 80 named lakes, well over half of them in *Pinecrest*.

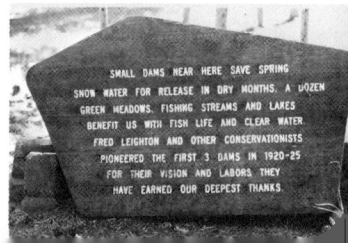

Glacial polish and striations — Jeff Schaffer

The Geology

THE SIERRA OF TODAY, considered by geologists to be a range in comparative infancy, was born over 200 million years (m.y.) ago! Then, a very shallow sea covered all of California, lapping against North American continental shores far to the east. While dinosaurs battled above, vast quantities of molten rock, called *magma*, migrated up through the earth's crust under California in giant liquid bubbles called *plutons*. Relatively little of the magma reached the surface. Most of it cooled several miles below the earth's surface, and in each pluton minerals slowly crystallized from the mixture to form one or another kind of granitic rock. The plutons that were created in this era, which lasted some 120 m.y., are collectively called the Sierra Nevada batholith. These granitic intrusions buckled the overlying strata, folding and squeezing the layers of sand, silt, limestone and volcanic sediments as if they were a giant accordion. The pressure and heat to which these sedimentary rocks were subjected altered their crystalline structure — that is, the pressure and heat *metamorphosed* the rocks.

Next came a long (40 m.y.) period of erosion. The Sierra region, slightly domed up by the granitic intrusions, had forced the Pacific Ocean west to the vicinity of the present-day Great Valley, so now the intensely folded metamorphic rocks were susceptible to the erosive action of wind, sun, frost and rain. By the end of this period, some 40 m.y. ago, most of the metamorphic layers had been removed from the Sierra dome, baring the granitic batholith. The last part of the erosive period was quite tropical, with much rain and lush vegetation. During this time, a thick, bright-red soil was formed by weathering of the rocks to clay and iron oxides (rust). One special mineral, however, was resistant to the weathering processes — gold. This very heavy element, formed in veins found in the upper batholith and the metamorphic rocks, was eroded from them and washed downstream to be redeposited at the base of the range. These rich alluvial deposits, called placers, would draw fortune seekers from around the world in the Gold Rush of 1849.

After the erosive epoch came a time of volcanic activity. This phase was marked by two types of extrusions — glowing avalanches and volcanic mudflows — plus lesser occurrences of lava flows. From vents near and east of the present Sierra crest, many cubic miles of hot volcanic ash cascaded down both slopes of the Sierra, completely burying the previous landscape. Ash eruptions were followed by denser volcanic rocks which, saturated with water, flowed as mudslides over the ash. Man's major interest in these ancient volcanic activities — remnants of which blanket the northern *Pinecrest* quad — is that they buried the river channels that contained placer gold.

Well into the phase of vulcanism, the Sierra began to tilt. Commencing some 10 m.y. ago, a massive fault block, composed of almost all the present-day Sierra and some land to its east, began to rotate upon an axis somewhere in the Great Valley. Commencing about 3 m.y. ago, mammoth cracks, or faults, developed along the top of the arched Sierra, and a huge block more or less dropped out of the arch to form the Owens Valley and other eastside valleys.

The final chapter of the Sierra's evolution to date is primarily a cosmetic one. Several million years ago there began a world-wide Ice Age, and glaciers covered the latitudinal extremes and the mountainous regions of the earth. In the Sierra Nevada, glaciers were so extensive that they coalesced into an octopuslike ice cap which, in *Pinecrest*, covered almost the entire area above 8000 feet. Glaciers that waxed and waned in the last 100,000 years were responsible for the deep U-shaped valleys, sparkling lakes and waterfalls, and mounds of till — a loose mix of boulders, sand and pebbles — found throughout the *Pinecrest* backcountry.

One will find three types of rocks in *Pinecrest*: intrusive, extrusive and metamorphic. The intrusive rocks, usually granites, and the extrusive rocks, which are derived from volcanic

The Geology

eruptions, belong to the igneous rock family, which encompasses all rocks formed from magma. The metamorphic rocks we see used to be another kind of rock, but heat and pressure altered them to their present state.

The intrusive rocks are of greatest interest to the Sierra traveler, for they make up most of the High Sierra. Molten magma, because of its relative lightness, rises to near the earth's surface, or, as extrusive rock, bursts upon it. This superheated fluid cools as it intrudes into existing rocks or is deposited on the surface, and its rate of cooling, combined with its final chemical makeup, determine what kind of igneous rock will form. Some minerals solidify at higher temperatures than others. In igneous rocks, these minerals are rich in iron, calcium and magnesium. These first minerals are usually darker and always denser than those that form at lower temperatures, such as quartz, which is the last mineral to form in granitic rocks. The heavier dark minerals, called *mafic* because of their high *ma*gnesium and iron (*Fe*) content, plus the lightweight and light-colored *felsic* minerals (high in *fel*dspar and *si*lica) result in the usual salt-and-pepper coloration and pattern of most Sierran intrusive rocks.

Different kinds of mafic and felsic minerals often group together, resulting in varying textures and colors of rock. They range from very felsic rocks to ultramafic ones. Granite and quartz monzonite are examples of felsic (high-quartz) rocks. True granite is uncommon in the Sierra, but much quartz monzonite is found. In the intermediate range lies granodiorite, quite common in *Pinecrest*, while the darker mafic rocks (little or no quartz) are diorite, gabbro and peridotite, outcrops of which are scattered throughout our quadrangle. Formed under conditions of higher temperature and pressure than felsic rocks, mafic rocks are more unstable at the low temperatures and pressure found at the earth's surface. This makes them weather more easily than the granites and granodiorites, as can be seen near Whitesides Meadow, or at 5600 feet in Cherry Creek Canyon. Here, as in other places throughout the quad, granodiorite stands obdurate against the elements while, close by, gabbroic rock crumbles to sand.

An observant traveler in *Pinecrest* will note that all the physical features of the landscape — cliffs, outcrops and valleys — are predetermined in their shape by two types of fracturing of the rock. The effects of the first kind, *jointing*, can be determined merely by looking at the *Pinecrest* topo map. Note how all the major canyons and their attendant ridges trend northeast/southwest, while most tributaries are at right angles to them. These large-scale features are controlled by granite's tendency to fracture along three planes, all at right angles to one another, forming solid rectangles.

The second type of fracturing, responsible more for smaller features — generally domes and cliffs — is called *exfoliation sheeting*. Exfoliation can be likened to the peeling of an onion, layer by layer. Huge, rounded sheets of granitic rock, from only inches to tens of feet thick, separate from the parent rock, and their departure gradually rounds it to form the numerous domes, large and small, and the sweeping cliffs that abound in the Emigrant Wilderness. The mechanism behind exfoliation is thought to involve the original crystalline structure of the rock as it cooled many miles beneath the surface. The crystals were arranged to withstand the incredible pressure at this great depth. Then, as weathering removed the overlying rock, the crystal structure, which was "pushing up" to support the overlying rock, no longer had so much weight above. Because of the internal pressures, the rock fractured roughly along the profile of the ground surface above it. Hence, exfoliation sheets that develop along a canyon's walls are roughly parallel to the walls, while those that form under a flat area are essentially horizontal.

The remaining features we see today were added by the Ice Age which began in the Sierra Nevada about 3 m.y. ago and *temporarily* ended about 10,000 years ago. Massive tongues of ice were the primary tools, emanating from cirques, which are ice-carved mountain hollows where snow accumulation ex-

Toms Canyon septum, Piute Meadow

Exfoliation on Peak 8240+ NNW of Wheeler Peak

ceeds melting. The Pinto Lakes bowl, the head of Post Corral Canyon, the head of Coolidge Meadow, and the trough in which Many Island Lake rests are examples of cirques. Glaciers had three basic tools with which to sculpt the landscape: rock debris, weight and momentum, and freezing. As the glacier moved, it picked up and carried with it loose rock fragments, ranging in size from sand grains to rocks the size of Greyhound busses. These rocks, embedded in the moving ice, chiseled, gouged, scratched and polished the underlying rocks. Long, parallel grooves, called striae and found throughout *Pinecrest*, indicate the direction of a glacier's flow. Where sand could do its work, the rock below was given a mirrorlike finish. Often, jointing or exfoliation features were so aligned that a glacier could tear off massive blocks or flakes. The rock was then frozen firmly into the glacier, as the ice flowed around it like taffy, and "plucked" it from the bedrock. Plucking is responsible for the alternation of steep faces and smooth flats that one sees while walking up any valley in the Emigrant Wilderness. Where rock was massive and resistant, the glacier could get no purchase, and its effort was expended in smoothing the surface. Wherever the glacier could grip an edge, however, it ripped up large chunks of rock. The French term *roches moutonées* is used for glacially scoured outcrops that show this action: smooth and gentle on the upstream side; rough, broken and steep-faced downstream. *Roches moutonées* are found throughout the *Pinecrest* region.

Extrusive igneous rocks, like the intrusives, range in chemical composition from high in quartz to lacking quartz. The difference between an extrusive rock and the corresponding intrusive rock is that the extrusive one cooled much more quickly on exposure to the air, and had very little time for crystals to grow. Silicon-rich quartz latite will be seen when climbing the 7200-foot ridge separating the Bell and Lily Creek waters on the Pine Valley Trail, while iron-rich andesite, a much more commonly seen volcanic rock of a grey to red-brown color, is found throughout *Pinecrest*'s volcanic outcrops. Most of the

The Geology

andesite is seen as a jumble of textures and colors mixed willy-nilly throughout a cementing mass, the result of volcanic mudslides. As this material was ejected from vents near the Sierra crest (near Relief Peak in our region), it mixed with water to flow as far as the Central Valley. This rock is called mudflow *breccia* (meaning made of fragments) or *agglomerate*. The earliest series of flows of this type in our area is called the Relief Peak Formation, and most of the volcanic rocks in *Pinecrest* are of this age (19-9 m.y. old). Castle Rock and the Three Chimneys are remnants of volcanic mudflows.

After the Relief Peak Formation was created, the Stanislaus Formation, whose quartz latite flows now form Tuolumne Table Mountain and the Dardanelles, was emplaced. Due to erosion, only a few pockets of this debris will be seen, some east of Bell Meadow.

A final point of interest in *Pinecrest*'s volcanic rocks is the presence underneath them of uranium-bearing minerals in the Niagara and Eagle Creek drainages. The largest uranium mine in California, the Juniper Mine, discovered in 1955, is located south of Sardine Meadow. Here, worked from a large open pit, uranium-bearing minerals named autunite, torbernite and uraninite are found in a black alluvium resting on granite.

We won't see many metamorphic rocks in the *Pinecrest* backcountry, but they are interesting enough to warrant mention. The major metamorphic feature of the western Emigrant Basin is the Toms Canyon septum, which runs discontinuously south from Whitesides Meadow to near Bourland Meadow. Septa, in the geologic sense, are remnants of metamorphic formations. In this case, all but scattered portions of the original rocks into which the Sierra Nevada batholith intruded and which it metamorphosed, have been eroded away. What remains consists of compactly folded rock ranging from dark, iron-rich *schist* (a fine-grained metamorphic rock that easily fractures along the old sedimentary layers) to light, silica-rich (SiO_2) *gneiss* (a coarse-grained granitic rock that has been compressed into layers). Mixed in and cutting through these metamorphic rocks are numerous dikes of very dark, coarse-grained ultramafic intrusive rock.

East Flange Rock from Lower Relief Valley

The Ecosystem

ECOLOGY, A WORD bandied about often in these days of oil crises and pollution, has a much gentler connotation to the wilderness enthusiast. Ecology is the study of the interworkings of the world's biotic (living) and abiotic (inorganic) communities. Multidisciplinary and loosely bounded, it lets the ecologist, the jack-of-all-trades of the natural sciences, borrow freely the ideas he wants from botany, zoology, meteorology, geology, and the behavioral sciences.

The ecologist's basic study unit is the community, or ecosystem. A community is all the animals and plants that live, die, eat each other, decompose, or excrete within a defined set of circumstances, such as their climate, the soil they live on, and the water they drink. Ecologists try to take into account everything in a certain area which affects its organisms, and, conversely, how the organisms affect the rocks, soil, water, etc.

In 1898 C. Hart Merriam divided North America into 7 broad ecosystems, which he called "life zones." These zones correspond roughly with latitude, from the Tropical Zone, which stretches from Florida across Mexico, to the Arctic Zone, which includes the polar regions. An interesting fact about these zones is that an increase in elevation has the same effect on the life zones as does moving north. A rise of 100 feet has roughly the same effect as going 17 miles north at the same altitude. Going up a mountain, therefore, could be similar to walking to Alaska, in terms of the changes in flora, fauna and climate. In the Sierra Nevada, one will, by climbing east to the crest from the foothills, traverse five life zones in less than 10,000 feet of elevation gain.

The life zones are defined, for convenience, mostly by plant species, which don't migrate and are therefore more indicative of the varying climatic conditions to which they must adapt. The life zones in *Pinecrest* are as follows:

Transition Zone (Yellow Pine Belt). The main timber region of the Sierra lies in this zone, above the Foothill (Upper Sonoran) Zone. It has pleasant summers but also receives the greatest amount of precipitation — up to 80 inches, much of it winter snows. In some cooler canyons, such as the Stanislaus's deep gorge, this zone extends down to 2000-foot altitude, but generally it starts near 3500 feet. Its upper limits reach 7200 feet in some places in *Pinecrest*, but it usually gives way to the Lodgepole/Red Fir Belt below 6500 feet.

Canadian Zone (Lodgepole/Red Fir Belt). Most of the *Pinecrest* backcountry lies in this high-mountain belt of lakes and glaciated granite. Here, above 6800 feet, the snow lingers late into summer, a boon for the winter-sports enthusiast but a hindrance to plant growth — the growing season lasts only the summer months. In *Pinecrest* this belt begins to mix with the Hudsonian close to the 8800-foot contour.

Hudsonian Zone (Subalpine Belt). Bracing air in all seasons and the nodding-topped spires of mountain hemlocks herald our passage into this ecosystem. Here the yearly precipitation is much less than in the lower zones, but nearly all of it is snow.

Arctic Zone (Alpine Belt). As the Hudsonian forest thins due to exposure to thinner air, shrill winds and killing ice, the plants shrink to lilliputian dimensions and crawl, prostrate, to the shelter of protective boulders or the lee of a ridge. Higher still, even these plants, and the animals that live with them, cannot cope with the intense cold, frozen ground, and a short growth period that might not even come at all in severe years. This is the realm of the specialists in alpine survival, those dwarfed plants and animals that have developed specialized bodies and eating habits for living in an adverse environment. The Alpine Belt is found in *Pinecrest* only in the northeast extreme of the quad, where Granite Dome and the volcanic eminences around Cooper Peak and East Flange Rock thrust above timberline.

Hikers in the *Pinecrest* backcountry will quickly note that the plants and animals in a life zone are not distributed uniformly, nor are the combinations of species living together in different climates totally different. Some plants and animals are always found together, or live in only one set of circumstances; others can be found all over *except* for one situation. Patterns soon become apparent, and these patterns are the basis for the subdivision of Life Zones into biotic communities. A biotic community is a unique combination, or association, of plants, animals, soil and environmental factors different from all other combinations of these things found in the broader life zone. For example, the Transition Zone is made up of a patchwork quilt of the following biotic communities: marshes, ponderosa forest, chaparral, mixed coniferous forest, lakes, transition zone meadows, and streamside communities.

Each biotic community has one, two, or a handful of species or environmental requirements which set it apart from all others. For example, each of the four life zones in *Pinecrest* has meadows of one sort or another, but the meadows differ in many respects. In the Transition Zone, meadows are characterized by lush grasses with some sedges, and a myriad of herbaceous annuals sporting diverse and colorful flowers. Hudsonian meadows are much less robust, although they share many species with the Transition Zone. Alpine Zone meadows are generally a mat of tough perennial shrubs and willows, with only a few tufts of hardy sedges. Some plants, and many animals, will overlap in either zonal or community affiliations. For example, Brewer's blackbirds range from low elevations to alpine climes, but are seen only in meadows. Robins are less particular whether they feed in meadow or forest, but they remain below the colder high country. Many predatory animals roam throughout the Sierra — for example, hawks, ravens and coyotes. But some predators are restricted, such as the small red fox, which patrols only the high country. Other animals, like the playful Oregon junco, will be seen anytime, anywhere. In the plant world, some genera are represented throughout *Pinecrest*, but by different though similar-looking species which reflect subtle ecological changes.

Let's look at the homes, habits and requirements of a sampling of typical *Pinecrest* flora and fauna, using an imaginary hike up the South Fork Stanislaus River which, in a 3900-foot ascent from 5621-foot Pinecrest Lake, touches all four life zones we'll see in our area.

Pinecrest Lake sits squarely in a classical Transition Zone Mixed Coniferous Forest. Our elevation here is just short of the zone of maximum precipitation, which averages some 55 inches annually. The combination of heavy precipitation and warm summers has created an ideal climate for a host of evergreens, which make up the bulk of the community. Ponderosa pine and white fir are the key species, but are usually found in combination with incense-cedar, sugar pine, black oak, and some Jeffrey pine. This mixture of tall conifers creates a high, open canopy which lets dappled light filter down to the mat of deep black humus and dead pine needles which cover the forest floor. An interesting group of plants find a home in this layer's deep shade. Called "saprophytes," they live solely on decaying vegetation and don't need or have chlorophyll to produce food. These bizarre plants, all of which have red coloration caused by hemoglobinlike fluids, sprout soon after the snow has melted. Snow plant, the most common saprophyte, has the appearance of a squat crimson asparagus. Pine drops is a cousin of snow plant, but has a thin, dull-red stalk reaching 3 feet in height from which hang globular flowers resembling Christmas ornaments on a sickly tree. If you come across sugar stick, you can count yourself very lucky. This gaudy specimen resembles nothing so much as a flowery candy cane!

But it is in the forest's vertical world that a visitor will see most of the Transition Zone's life. Hundreds of species of birds and a number of mammals make their homes almost exclusively in the forest canopy. In the birds, in particular, one will note specializations that keep all species from competing with each other. Clownlike chickadees, tiny birds with tinier voices and black burglar's masks, frolic in groups only near the ends of branches, obtaining insect dinners by means of gravity-defying acrobatics. On the tree trunks, feeding is even more specialized — the brown creeper, a homely bird with a long, curving beak, goes *up* the tree to gather meals, while the red-breasted nuthatch, with a slaty-blue back, black cap, and white underpinnings, searches for insects only while heading *down* the trunk!

General custodian and trouble maker of the Transition Zone avian world is the crusty, jaunty Steller jay, which flits about in pelage of bright blue and a charcoal-crested cowl. This jay roams throughout the Transition Zone, from forest to meadow to chaparral, but confines himself to that altitude; he's replaced by scrub jays lower down and by Clark nutcrackers higher up. An interesting habit is his method of ascending a tree — he hops up from branch to branch in spiral-staircase fashion.

Chickarees, small squirrels resplendent in neat coats of grizzled brown above and tan below, separated by a flashy black racing stripe, are the mammalian farmers of the Transition forest. A true denizen of the high canopy, a chickaree will seldom leave the trees except to retrieve and bury the pine cones that he acrobatically harvests from swaying perches at the ends of long limbs. Some of the cones are stripped and eaten just after cutting, leaving "cone cobs" and piles of empty scales lying at a conifer's base. Not hibernators, these furry dynamos are active most any winter's day, and use their acute olfactory sense to seek out their caches of cones. But they're not infallible, so many food piles go uneaten, and from them trees are born. Chickarees have but a small reputation for sociability. Upon an invasion of his small aerial fiefdom, real or imagined, a chickaree will scuttle down a trunk to engage in a long-winded tirade of apoplectic coughs and staccato cries. He'll maintain this uproar until the intruder departs, at which time he might lapse into less convulsive mutterings, often lasting long after the incident!

While walking around Pinecrest Lake, one cannot help but notice that the north shore is more brushy and open than the south shore, which is almost uniformly clad in forest. The vegetational differences between the north and south sides of the entire Stanislaus River canyon are due to differing amounts of received sunlight. On Pinecrest Lake's north shore, sunlight and its attendant heating and drying effects are almost too much to allow a growth of conifers — only Jeffrey pines, more properly members of the Canadian Zone, are found sparsely dotting the slopes. But the hillside is far from bare. These hot exposures are an ideal situation for chaparral, which in the Transition Zone is made up of huckleberry oaks, black oaks, gold-cup oaks, manzanita, chinquapin and ceanothus. This impenetrable thicket is an entirely different environment, caused by different soil (it's dry and sandy, without the forest's humus), temperatures and terrain. Birds suited to long glides in an open forest can't navigate in these brushy confines, so green-tailed towhees and fox sparrows, which have stubbier wings and ground-feeding habits, take their place.

Moving up through the meadows above Pinecrest Lake, we note more and more Jeffrey pines and an occasional lodgepole pine, sure indications that we're entering the Canadian Zone. As we've climbed, we've noticed that flower species that have bloomed and died below are either still blooming or are not even opened up yet at this altitude. This phenomenon is example of another precept of the life-zone hypothesis. Not only does life change with elevation and altitude, but also with time of year. Winter comes first to the higher elevations, and thaws set in first at the lower elevations. In general, seasonal change, blooming times, and insect hatches follow this rule: one day equals 100 feet in elevation. So if corn lily blossoms on May 30 at Pinecrest Campground, it will blossom about June 17th at Waterhouse Lake, 1800 feet higher. As we climb, we're going back to earlier in the season, from the ecological viewpoint.

First Forest, at 6200 feet, is our first look at a Canadian Zone flora. We'll note, coming into it, that this Canadian Zone community is like a finger pointing down the Stanislaus River canyon, surrounded by Transition Zone life. The boundaries of life zones and communities are never distinct, because a change in conditions is rarely abrupt. So where warm slopes prevail at a higher altitude than normal, a "lower" community will be found next to life more accurately reflecting the elevation. And the reverse is true, as here — in river canyons and on north-facing slopes, higher-type life can take advantage of cooler conditions and extend into lower altitudes.

The Canadian Zone is exemplified by two very different floral and faunal combinations, each due to a different environment. The lodgepole-pine forest, which we'll see so much of up-canyon, is the commoner of the two. In Second Forest, we are in the red-fir community, a valuable lumbering community. Here, the firs' dark canopy screens out so much light that the only plants able to grow below are saprophytes, like coral root, in the shadows, or bracken fern along the stand's margin. Where no plants grow, there are no animals. In a red-fir forest, animal life is restricted primarily to the overstory.

As we walk along the South Fork, it's obvious that the communities in the canyon don't come right down to its edge. Instead, there is another community that parallels the streamside. Frequently it has many of the plants found in adjoining communities — willows, grasses, spiraea and ferns — but the dominant species — quaking aspen, cottonwood and alder — occur only near water. Certain animals have become quite at home in this interface of water and land. Yellow-legged frogs, the most common Sierran amphibian, hunt for stream-dwelling insects, and seek shelter in exfoliation crevices when disturbed. Strangely enough, these frogs' competition comes from a bird. Though related to thrushes, the water ouzel, or dipper, shares few of his ancestors' habits. This little slate-grey bird is completely at home *under* the water! Using a pair of oversize feet and a unique waterproof pelage, the ouzel walks right into cascades in search of its favorite food, the caddis-fly nymph. Not only can it walk underwater, but it frequently *flies* in these chilly pools, using its strong, stubby wings. Final proof of this

Mature silver pines — a red-fir associate *Jeff Schaffer*

The Ecosystem

bird's overwhelming affinity for water is its choice of nesting sites — right behind a waterfall, where the spray keeps its moss-lined nest damp!

By the time we reach Waterhouse Lake the second basic community making up the Lodgepole/Red Fir Belt has taken over. Lodgepole pines are the order of the day, almost to the exclusion of other species. The ecological composition of this community is determined primarily by the density of lodgepole pines. Where trees are sparse and soil is relatively lacking, as on slabby granitic bedrock, only streptanthus, pussy paws or mouse-tailed ivesia grows sparingly in patches of gruss soil. When conditions are better, on a deep soil with plenty of moisture, there might be a nearly inpenetrable thicket of young trees. Numerous shrubs, such as spiraea, rose and mat manzanita, will be found in these forests, along with a variety of annuals. Corn lily is the most common, with yarrow, yellow violets, and false Solomon's seal in accompaniment. Corn lily will be seen ringing almost every meadow in the Canadian Zone, intermingled with clumps of young lodgepole pines. This classical pattern of meadow enroachment by these pines is hastened by overgrazing by cattle and especially pack stock, which are frequently thoughtlessly and illegally picketed in these delicate grasslands. Once the slow-growing meadow turf has been disturbed, ideal conditions are created for corn lily, which in turn alters the soil to the benefit of lodgepole pines.

The most common inhabitant of any meadowed patch in the Canadian Zone is the little gray-brown Belding ground squirrel, or "picket pin." These gregarious rodents, about rat-size, dwell in labrynthine tunnels, their entrances usually concealed by overhanging grasses. The approach of a hiker, or any assumed predator, to the abode of a Belding is first signalled by an upright "picket pin" stance, then by a shrill whistle which sends his fellows scurrying for their holes. Along with meadow mice, these rodents are low men on the food-chain totem pole, and hawks, snakes, weasels, martens, coyotes and badgers assure the average picket-pin of but a short life span.

Gopher "ropes" at Wilson Meadow Lake

The Ecosystem

When we reach Cooper Meadow, we note a change in the character of the meadow growth. The most obvious difference in this meadow's make-up is that the soil it grows on is primarily volcanic alluvium, washed down from the mud-flow battlements of Castle Rock and the Three Chimneys. In volcanic-soil meadows, both the texture and the type of plants differ from those in granitic-soil meadows. In granite sand, the grass cover is nearly uniform and thick, forming a turf of grasses, sedges and moisture-loving annuals like buttercup, gentian, violet, shooting star and aster. Volcanic meadows, however, have an appearance of anemia, with much bare earth showing between tufted vegetation. No doubt the hundreds of pocket gophers which call these meadows home are a contributing factor, for mounds of earth marking the entrances to their tunnels and crisscrossing "gopher ropes" — cylindrical cores of soil deposited by the gophers as they tunneled through winter snows — are found throughout these grasslands.

Leaving Cooper Meadow on our way to Cooper Pocket, we might note curious horizontal rows of welts on the bark of some lodgepole pines. These pits are the work of Williamson's sapsuckers, specialists among woodpeckers who drink the tree's sap as well as the odd ant or bit of cambium caught in the sticky liquid.

Our encounter with Hudsonian (Subalpine) Zone species in the South Fork Stanislaus River is a short one. This zone fingers down into Cooper Pocket almost to 8600 feet, and ends at timberline near 9400 feet. It is typified by one tree in the *Pinecrest* area — mountain hemlock. Preferring colder northern exposures where snow lingers late into summer, this tree sometimes grows tall in barren-floored forests, and sometimes in a more stunted form in isolated rock perches. Characteristics of this species are branches almost to the ground, numerous immature trees forming bowers (excellent for camping) around a larger hemlock's base, and extremely flexible branches, which can bend under heavy snows without breaking.

Flitting among the hemlocks one will see a raucous, assertive bird called the Clark nutcracker. A large relative of jays and crows, he surveys his montane domain from the apex of a strategic conifer. He is, like his kin, catholic in tastes and adept as a plunderer, but his specialty is cracking hard green pine cones, for which he has developed a strong, sharp, black beak.

As mountain hemlock exemplifies the Hudsonian Zone's conifers, the indicative ground cover of the zone consists of two similar shrubs — red and white heather. These wiry perennials, which grow separately or together to form foot-high mats wherever soil and moisture permit, have among the prettiest flowers to be seen at high altitudes. Their bell-shaped blossoms attract rufus and calliope hummingbirds, both of which visit these altitudes in summer.

Our climb out of Cooper Pocket witnesses a thinning of the hemlock overstory until only scattered specimens dot a jumble of broken granite and brown volcanic slope wash. The rock piles are a favored home of the Sierra's largest rodent, the yellow-bellied marmot. About the size of an overfed domestic cat and with the carriage of a badger, a marmot suns his grizzled yellow-brown coat on a protected rock or from a meadow viewpoint. Sometimes hibernating for almost nine months out of the year, marmots emerge in early summer and quickly make up for lost feeding time. By the end of summer, most marmots have taken on a decided Churchillesque bearing, and some can't even keep their yellow stomachs from dragging on the ground between their stubby legs! When alarmed, these somnolent creatures rouse themselves to their haunches and let forth a shrill warning whistle before plunging into a den among the talus.

Finally, we emerge on the nearly treeless volcanic ridge east of Cooper Pocket, at an elevation of over 9450 feet. We stand on the lower margin of the highest Sierran life zone, the Alpine Zone. A few trees are scattered about, mostly white bark pines, a hardy species that can weather the biting winds that frequently drop the temperature below zero and deposit thick

The Ecosystem

ice rimes that glaze and kill leaves and branches. The plants that survive here are of two types: perennials which have found sheltered microclimates that keep the elements' full intensity from afflicting them; and delicate annuals that dare to sprout only in the few weeks of summer when the weather is least inhospitable.

All the plants here owe their existence to a much smaller organism found crusting the rocks in splashes of green, gray, black, red, orange, chartreuse or lemon-yellow. Called a lichen, it is actually two separate plants growing in a mutual-benefit relationship. The main body is a fungus, while embedded in it are algal cells which, through their possession of food-producing chlorophyll, make food for themselves and the fungus. The fungus provides the algae with minerals from the rock and water from the air. Although lichens work and grow with painful slowness, they inexorably decompose the rock surfaces they cling to and thus gradually develop a soil suitable for plant growth. Almost impervious to cold, rain and solar radiation, these minute crusts here coat everything from autobrecciated boulders down to tiny pebbles in a blaze of lemon yellows and fiery reds to shout their eventual domination over even this most hostile landscape.

The Arctic Zone is often called "the Alpine desert," for it receives so little precipitation, most of it snow quickly evaporated to the cold dry air by shrieking winds. And when water does reach plants' roots, they can't pick it up — it is too cold to be taken into their vascular systems. But, as in the hot desert, plants and animals in the Alpine desert have made special adaptations to this cold world of little water. Plants waste little energy or fluid on yearly growth or elaborate flowers that might be killed in a sudden frost. Like desert species, some plants here have developed waxy coatings and smaller leaves to prevent water loss. Other plants, like hulsea, ivesia and sky pilot, have gone another route, repeatedly dissecting their feathery leaves so that the copious evaporation of water off the leaves forcibly "pulls" water up through their roots.

Generally, all plants here are small, hunched to the wind and cold. Sagebrush and mule ears, which favor volcanic soil at any altitude, are the largest species here, but much smaller than their cousins lower down. Fireweed, which grew to 6 feet near Pinecrest, can't live at this altitude, but a diminutive member of the same genus, rockfringe, bears its beautiful pink flowers in the protection of rock niches.

Only the smaller rodents make this place home. Most of them hibernate through the bitter winter, coming out when flowers put forth a brief, colorful flurry of blossoms and seeds. This short period attracts numerous seed-eating birds, notably sparrows, and mule deer, who come up from winter bivouacs in lower climes to sample the sweet grasses. And the coyote is always where the action is, waiting patiently on the side lines with his aerial counter part, the red-tailed hawk, for any animal, from mouse to deer, to make a mistake or show signs of weakness.

Bennett juniper, a dry-soil tree

The Trails

ANY WILDERNESS ENTHUsiast, from novice to seasoned trail-pounder, with a short weekend, a whole vacation, or only a few hours at his disposal can find enjoyment among the glistening domes, deep canyons, quiet lakes, and forest-clad ridges in the *Pinecrest* backcountry. The routes described in this guide are of three types: main trails, laterals and cross-country routes. Choosing one of the main trails, one can then add side hikes along laterals or cut across to another main trail to exit from the wilderness via another route, making a loop trip, the most effective way to spend one's all-too-short time in this beautiful subalpine wonderland. There are trips to please anglers, loafers, botanists, children, and rugged types looking for a strenuous workout.

Main Trails. These are the major arterials that penetrate to the heart of the Emigrant Wilderness and carry most of the traffic, horse and pedestrian. In general, they are well-maintained by Forest Service trail crews, are signed at trail junctions, and are well-traveled enough that novices should not hesitate to embark on them.

Lateral Trails. Ranging in length from only a fraction of a mile to many miles, these trails can be used to join main trails into loop trips or to reach lakes for base-camped explorations or for merely an overnight stay. Some laterals are as well-kept as main trails, while others are nothing more than use trails marked by blazes or ducks. (*Blazes* are rectangular patches of bark removed from trees at eye level. *Ducks* are small rocks, usually two or three, piled one on the other in an obviously unnatural manner. *Cairns* are larger rock piles).

Cross-Country Routes. Sooner or later, hikers who find even the Emigrant Wilderness' beaten paths too tame and who have the requisite experience will choose a cross-country hike, where the route can be varied at will to suit one's desire for challenges. In *Pinecrest* the cross-country enthusiast has a bonanza. Almost any canyon or ridge that doesn't already have a trail can be easily walked, because of the open nature of the granitic terrain. Some of the best cross-country routes, which ascend viewful peaks, wind down meadowed valleys, or strike off to reach remote and well-stocked tarns, are described in this guide, but competent trekkers needn't be restricted to them. Many of the cross-country routes are no more difficult than a trail except that you must follow a compass bearing to reach your destination. Some of the cross-country hikes described here, however, pose demanding route-finding problems or short rock-scrambling difficulties and should be attempted only by experienced hikers.

Sardella Lake, Relief Peak from Granite Dome

Trail Descriptions

MAIN TRAIL #1

Kibbie Ridge Trail: Cherry Dam to Huckleberry Lake
(Trail 20E11)

(**Roadend:** To reach the Cherry Valley Dam parking area, turn onto Road 1N07 at a point on State Highway 120 about 15 miles east of Groveland, then continue 24 miles to a signed parking area just west of Cherry Valley Dam. An alternate, possibly faster route for those coming from north of Highway 120 is to follow Road 1N04 from the town of Tuolumne, which joins Road 1N07 just yards before the parking area at Cherry Dam.)

From the parking area, located in a dusty mixed coniferous forest at 4780 feet just west of the south end of Lake Lloyd, popularly known as Cherry Lake, we clamber up a short slope or follow the short parking spur road back to Road 1N07, which winds down past some houses to 2600-foot-long Cherry Valley Dam. Walking northeast along a road topping the 330-foot-high impoundment, we gaze north over the clear blue waters of this huge 268,000 acre-foot reservoir to the granite domes dimpling Cherry Creek Canyon. Our elevation at spillway level is only 4700 feet, and we find ourselves in a dry Transition Zone forest of ponderosa pine, black oak and incense-cedar, with much manzanita inhabiting the sunnier places. Turning north on a dirt road at Cherry Dam's east end, we stroll through this forest, which is floored with fragrant kit-kit-dizze, abundant shield-leaved streptanthus, and dainty purple and yellow mimulus. Our road contours above an old, now-little-used trail; then, as we dip down toward the reservoir, the trail crosses our route, signed for Kibbie Ridge, Lake Eleanor and Lords Meadow.

This trail, which we take, winds above the lakeshore, sometimes far enough back in now-denser trees to obscure our view of it, then turns northeast to a thick stand of incense-cedar, where the Lake Eleanor Trail branches southeast. Crossing an oiled gravel road and a spring-fed rivulet, and ascending a small granite knoll via a gentle-to-moderate ascent, we hit a wide, gravelled road at 4980 feet. The trail's junction with this road (1N45Y) is rather vague, and hikers headed in either direction should be sure to angle across this road. In an open forest of gold-cup and black oaks we switchback on a northward course over bouldery till along the west slope of Kibbie Ridge, sometimes perceiving blue fragments of Cherry Lake and signs of a huge burn on the ridge to its west, through a now-thicker forest of Jeffrey pine and white fir. These infrequent vistas are only partial consolation for the steep, dusty ascent, often on deep sand, with ample evidences of past logging operations. We

Looking north from summit of Mercur Peak. Note joint control of landscape.

have one respite — at 5440 feet, two small springs emerge just above our route, watering lady ferns, bracken and tiger lilies, and supplying droughts of cold water — before we're forced to resume our ascent. Just over one mile later we halt again, to sample the pleasures of Shingle Spring, situated in a ravine shaded by white fir, Jeffrey pine and dogwood, and giving water from a wooden horse-trough. Adequate camping can be had below the path.

Continuing on, our feet lead up rotting granite slabs to a ridgetop covered by manzanita and chinquapin, then gently down into cool Deadhorse Gulch, drained by a trickling creek in early summer. Soon we pass a junction with the Kibbie Lake Trail, going northeast, and then wind gently north on duff past a shallow, weedy pond. Dropping past signed Sand Canyon, unrecognizable as such, but the location for a snow-survey plot and a rain gauge, we pass, in quick succession, a

marshy flat, a mapped creek with good camp, and a switchback which leads up onto sparsely forested granite slabs covered with "gruss," or granite sand. Note how the massive roots of the Jeffrey pines loosen and crush the peeling rock, hastening the development of soil. Drought-tolerant streptanthus, dwarf lupine, and sulfur-flower, plus lizards and pocket gophers, are the only visible species presently able to exist on this seemingly sterile surface. A sign pointing west to a helispot on a knoll signals a side excursion for good views of Cherry Lake, the Cherry Ridge Burn, and the high ranges south of Hetch Hetchy.

Our route re-enters red-fir forest, mixed with some white fir and Jeffrey pine, climbing steadily to signed Lookout Point, 7120'. Awesome vistas of granite cliffs and domes in the deep cleft of Cherry Creek Canyon can best be had by dropping 50 feet down into the huckleberry-oak scrub west of the path. From Lookout Point, we pant up an exposed, moderate pitch, quite dusty from stock use, finding occasional andesitic boulders transported here by glacial action. We then ease out in fir forest, now with much lodgepole, past Swede's Camp — a corn-lily-filled meadow — and ascend to a large, shallow pond. After skirting the sandy north shore of this warm lakelet, we climb under sparse mixed trees, often at a steep incline, to an open ridgetop sand flat and the Yosemite National Park boundary. Our steep, vague path straight up the sandy ridge, blessed with fine panoramas southeast to Mt. Conness and other peaks of the Tuolumne Meadows region, leads to the muddy, marsh-marigold-dotted terrain surrounding Sachse Spring. A good camp is found here in serene red-fir and lodgepole forest.

East of Sachse Spring, the trail undulate on morainal material in well-spaced western white pine and red fir. A large lakelet almost 0.2 mile north of the trail affords very good, but littered, camping on its south side. Beyond a seasonal creek, our route begins to descend onto open granite slabs, a harbinger of typical Emigrant Basin terrain to come. Mercur Peak,

Many Island Lake seen from the north

8080+, a prominent granite dome in the northeast, is a good showpiece of the two dominant erosional processes in this part of the Sierra — exfoliation ("onion-skin" rock peeling) and glaciation. Coming off the slabs into a small lodgepole forest surrounding a brown tarn, we keep right, following blazed trees and ducks, then continue on a bearing straight for Mercur Peak over sandy slabs. Mercur Peak, an easy scrambling ascent via the south slope, provides a fine vantage point for examining the southern Emigrant Basin. South of Mercur Peak, in lodgepole forest, we pass a large tarn, quite wet in early season around the camps on its north side, which marks the turnoff point for Many Island Lake.

To reach aptly named Many Island Lake, proceed due south through lodgepoles and around numerous early-season ponds to the low-angle slabs bounding the north part of the granite cirque that contains this glacial lake. By keeping one's feet flat on the sloping rock and pointed downhill, one should have no difficulty descending to the campsites flanking its warm, shallow waters.

East of the junction with the Many Island Lake cross-country route, the Kibbie Ridge Trail passes through a narrow, joint-controlled gully to unsigned Styx Pass, where we leave Yosemite National Park. We descend to better views of the North and East Fork Cherry Creek drainages, flanked by soaring domes and bosses. Eight tight, rocky switchbacks decorated by clumps of sedge and red Sierra onion bring us to a long traverse east to the Boundary Lake Trail, 0.6 mile from Styx Pass. The unsigned Boundary Lake Trail can be readily identified by its proximity to a double-trunked silver lodgepole snag. A long switchback leg completes our downgrade to Cherry Creek, where we enter a dense forest of lodgepole flanked on the south by a broad exfoliation dome and its talus, and on the north by very wide, green Cherry Creek. A fine technical climbing dome, Peak 7604, lies north of the creek. In Lord Meadow, the soggy lowland east of the confluence of the two forks of Cherry Creek, we encounter lodgepoles, mosquitos, muddy early-season detours, deer tracks, one good camp, one packer camp, and an easy, 80-foot-long crotch-deep (in early season) wade of East Fork Cherry Creek on sand and cobbles. About 150 feet after Cherry Creek, in a now-familiar type of open flat of slabs, gruss and huckleberry oak, we come to an unmarked junction with the North Fork Cherry Creek Trail. The ducked North Fork Trail here begins north, then goes west around lodgepoles below a 40-foot granite outcrop, while our route along the East Fork has a bearing of due east.

Walking off the slabs, we climb gently, alternating through wooded and open stretches, often near the cascading creek and its streamside accompaniment of lupine, bitter cherry, spireia, serviceberry and willow, to a tricky ford to the south side of East Fork Cherry Creek. Poorly situated just below a series of cascades, the 15-foot crossing is deep and fast over large, slick boulders. Hikers should avoid this crossing at high water by using the Cross-Country Alternate along the north side of Cherry Creek.

North Side Cherry Creek Cross-Country Alternate Route: West to East:

In times of high water it is better to avoid the second and third fords of Cherry Creek. You can do so by taking a cross-country route that leaves the trail about 75 yards before the second crossing. Bear left, northeast, avoiding huckleberry oak, to enter a bare glaciated bowl, the lip of which overlooks rapids above the second ford. A short pitch of class 1-2 scrambling to the top of a broad flat dome finishes the difficulties, from which the Huckleberry Lake Trail is rejoined a few hundred yards to one's east.

While taking a few minutes on the south side to dry feet and shoes, one might keep an eye out for mountain chickadees, juncos, steller jays, robins and violet-green swallows — the most common birds in this area. Dynamited switchbacks amid a riot of wildflowers lead us above foaming white cascades; then we contour back to the creekside, just above a large pool where we tread water-worn exfoliation shells to a triple-trunked lodgepole snag which indicates yet another crossing of East Fork Cherry Creek. Here the sliding stream is gentler, allowing an easy but slippery ford. Our route then cuts cross-slope under a fine 5th Class dome on slabs covered with exfoliation debris from across the canyon. This debris is ample evidence that avalanches can cross creeks and even move uphill. Ending the traverse, we come to a steep, gravelly climb on switchbacks to a small nose where we meet the North Side Cross-Country Alternate Route. Now in a broad, sparsely wooded glacial hanging valley, we climb more gently past mauve, shreddy-barked Sierra junipers, and come to a barren, glacially polished exfoliation surface, sprinkled with rounded erratic boulders and dimpled by smooth solution pockets. This bowl precedes the low saddle just west of Pruitt Lake creek.

To reach Pruitt Lake, bear north from this saddle for about 200 feet of moderate gain before swinging away to

East Fork Cherry Creek just east of *Pinecrest* **quad** *Jeff Schaffer*

avoid huckleberry-oak thickets on sloping slabs. Near Pruitt Lake's outlet it is possible to return to the creek. The deep, blue, rough rectangle of Pruitt Lake is nestled in groves of lodgepole and western white pines alternating with granite slabs from which diving and swimming are enjoyable. Rainbow trout to 8″ are numerous.

From the glaciated col marking the way to Pruitt Lake, the East Fork Trail makes a pair of switchbacks to hop across Pruitt Lake creek, then ascends close to the rocky banks of dancing Cherry Creek, with violet-green swallows swooping and gliding overhead to capture dinner — mostly mosquitos in

June and July. Our way skirts the south side of a glaringly polished dome, returning to the chuting rock trough of Cherry Creek, and comes into pastoral groves of mat manzanita and lodgepole pine under an awesome 5th Class and Aid face on the 400-foot dome to our northwest.

A winding, imperceptible ascent soon brings us to a snow-survey cabin, good campsites, and a junction with the Horse Meadow Trail, all of these beside broad, smooth-running Cherry Creek. As we continue along Cherry Creek's north bank, the sandy terrain is frequently thicketed with immature lodgepoles, and there are fine views west to the vertical dome face. Then, walking levelly, we come to a junction, at the southwest end of Huckleberry Lake, with a short lateral to the Horse Meadow Trail. Huckleberry Lake is a surprisingly clear 200-acre expanse of granite- and lodgepole-rimmed blue water, with camping possibilities on duff and mat manzanita around much of its shore. The generally shallow lagoons at its south end offer pleasant swimming, and abundant rainbow and brook trout live here.

Southwest end of Huckleberry Lake

MAIN TRAIL #2

Pine Valley Trail: Bell Meadow to Huckleberry Lake
(Trail 20E17)

(**Roadend:** Turn from State Highway 108 one mile east of Cold Springs onto Road 4N26 and follow it to a signed junction with Road 4N25. Take 4N25 1/3 mile southwest to a junction, and go right, east, on 4N20Y, which curves down to the large Bell Meadows parking area in a sandy lodgepole forest.)

Following trail signs east from the roadend, we skirt south of granitic outcrops, some good for rock climbing, on a deep, sandy tread, alternately through lodgepole groves and open spaces until we come upon the north margin of Bell Meadow. Level going brings us to two gorges deeply incised in the sandy alluvium by Bell Creek. Infrequent glimpses of massive Bell Mountain in the south are had through dark coniferous timber as our route climbs gently south, then undulates to a good campsite north of the trail at a step-across ford of the east fork of Bell Creek. Tank up on water here, for a hot, exposed climb ensues.

Climbing steeply in a gully notable for some large ponderosa pines, we soon arrive at a junction with the Mud Lake Trail, which climbs south through thick volcanic dust. Our way veers north to steeply ascend a cobbly nose, then alters to a fairly consistent moderate grade over rough volcanic rock. In the welcome shade of Jeffrey pines and white firs atop this 7200-foot divide we lower our gears for a hot, knee-numbing, switchbacking drop on nearly barren volcanic conglomerate to a lateral to Crabtree Camp. Dropping gently east into well-named Pine Valley — almost all lodgepoles — we come very soon to another trail south to Mud Lake. From this junction we ascend imperceptibly through open forest to cross the Bear Lake fork of Lily Creek via either a rock-hop or, earlier in the year, a knee-deep wade. A good campsite precedes that ford; an even better one lies just past it.

Trail Descriptions

Entering the Emigrant Wilderness, we come into more open terrain, with short lodgepoles, pussy paws, huckleberry oak, and other manifestations of dryness growing abreast of the trail. Reaching Grouse Lake, our route bisects a large camping complex on its north shore. Amateur naturalists who brave the hordes here — people and mosquitos — will find numerous plant and animal species, including an occasional bear, plus rainbow and brook trout. Just a bit farther on, we track north of the east arm of Grouse Lake, which also has good camps. The conspicuous rings of small holes in the bark of aspen trees in this area are caused by yellow-bellied sapsuckers; those in lodgepole pines are the work of Williamson's sapsuckers.

Grouse Lake

At the head of Grouse Lake we cross to the south shore of Lily Creek by log and resume the gentle eastward ascent, now in an ever-narrowing canyon. The higher we climb up this granitic cleft, the steeper and taller the cliffs become, and the rougher and rockier the path grows. Finally, close under a 500-foot-high face that looms in the south, we are forced to tread gray talus blocks, and the ascent becomes steep, hot and monotonous except for the surprising array of shrubs — huckleberry oak, manzanita, ceanothus, twinberry, ocean spray, currant, bitter cherry, serviceberry, willow, shrubby spiraea and gooseberry. Our climb does get gentler past isolated junipers near the bluffed pass dividing Piute from Lily Creek waters. A short distance beyond the saddle, an easy descent brings us to campsites at the crossing of Piute Creek. We quickly leave behind the little-used Studhorse Meadow Trail on the right, then the Piute Meadow lateral on the left, before rounding south into barren Groundhog Meadow. One might hear the thumping mating call of blue grouse here, a ventriloqual sound which, one must assume, can be traced by the female!

We continue moderately up into a fine mixed coniferous forest, past blossoms of senecio and lupine under the somber face of Peak 8124 to yet another col. Then, descending east, the path emerges from red fir at a rocky overlook from which upper Louse Canyon and the convergence of West Fork Cherry Creek and Buck Meadow Creek appear below. The entire scene is dominated by the gray visage of Point 8240+, which stands southeast of the bare granite amphitheater formed by the juncture of the two creeks, and would offer fine technical climbing up to two pitches long. This vista point marks a return to drier, more rocky going, and our route switchbacks dustily down through huckleberry oak and phlox to a junction from which a trail going southwest to Rosasco Lake passes a number of campsites just downstream. Early in the year, the ford of Cherry Creek immediately beyond this junction is a bit tricky, but it can be accomplished dry if you head upstream for a few yards to where boulders lead across the braided waters. Once more ascending, we traverse diorite slabs, following ducks across the monolithic rock, which shows glacial polish and striations. Considering that the highly polished surface was created by glaciers at least ten thousand years ago, it is in a remarkable state of preservation.

Gaining altitude via short, bouldery switchbacks on the north side of Buck Meadow Creek, the early-summer hiker will be presented with a multi-hued array of wildflowers — more than 20 species! The trail undulates over cobbled moraine, then switchbacks steeply up a bulging dioritic dome. A waterfall here attests to the stream's inability to erode this obstruction. Soon we come to the Gem Lake lateral, cross the outlet stream of that lake, and follow jointing fractures down to a boulder crossing of Buck Meadow Creek 100 feet upstream from the trail. A quick switchback in a duff-floored mountain-hemlock grove gives us a good look at the *roche moutonee* which stands across canyon. The low roar of frothing water accompanies us along Buck Meadow Creek until we begin to climb away from its banks into deep hemlock forest. Features to our north include the dome south of Jewelry Lake, which would offer several pitches of severe climbing.

At a point where we level out under a granitic nose and begin to drop, the cross-country route to Coyote Lake turns off southwest. A short distance beyond, we leap from rock to rock to cross Buck Meadow Creek, switchback quickly up and around a granite boss, cross the creek again via a large log-jam, and arrive at a junction with a lateral trail to Deer Lake. Only a few feet later we come into a large, damp, well-littered camping area at the west end of Wood Lake. Western tanagers, robins or varied thrushes might serenade us as we pause to lunch beside the shallow blue waters, gazing east to the horizon of Bigelow Peak. This 12-acre, 27-foot-deep, dumbbell-shaped lake offers very good angling for rainbow trout to 15″.

Passing along the willow-obscured south shore, we turn south into a shallow gully from where the Karls Lake Trail heads southwest to solitude and good fishing. From this junction, we tread on spongy loam past fine campsites nestled in hemlocks along the wide "canal" joining the lobes of Wood Lake. Rounding the shallower east lobe, we come to a sign that points incongruously east, right across Wood Lake, indicating *Main Trail*! Early in the season it would seem a dubious enterprise indeed to follow this advice, though the route is soddenly passable later in the year. A better route, though longer by 0.2 mile, is to follow the trail south around the water, passing a cluster of camps in a group of lodgepoles, and continue up a wooded gully, then go down to meet the main trail one third of the way east along the south shore of a yellow-pond-lilied tarn. This junction is marked well by ducks, so that those headed west may easily avoid a wade of Wood Lake.

Soon after this pond we find the Buck Lakes Trail at the lodgepole-shaded head of an 8400-foot saddle, where our route switchbacks east down among steep boulders and huckleberry oak. Near 8000 feet we bend south, then north back into forest at a sandy linkage with the Emigrant Lake/North Fork Trail beside musical North Fork Cherry Creek. Our route crosses Cherry Creek here via two 25-foot log traverses, then winds past morainal tarns to the north shore of Cow Meadow Lake. Tight, rocky switchbacks, with occasional views of the many lagoons of Cow Meadow Lake, lead 600 feet up into mountain-hemlock forest and to a gap where our route passes the Lertora Lake Trail. Douglas Lake, a small, rectangular, granite-bound tarn fringed with labrador tea, red heather and lodgepole, is skirted on the north as Trail 20E17 bends south toward the southwest end of Huckleberry Lake. Douglas Lake provides good brook-trout angling, fine swimming, and the best campsites for miles around.

Continuing on, we wind gently down a joint-fractured valley, crossing the small stream therein many times, then turn east to switchback down to a mosquitoey lakelet, often glimpsing Bigelow and Haystack Peaks, eastward in northern Yosemite. The final descent to Huckleberry Lake is negotiated by often-steep switchbacks in rocky, joint-controlled gullies, surrounded by huckleberry oaks and scattered lodgepoles. Surprising the hiker who expects another shallow, grassy mud puddle, Huckleberry Lake has clean blue waters enveloped in white rocks dotted with lodgepole groves, covering 200 acres to a depth of as much as 51 feet. As our trail winds south along narrow arms of the lake, camping is possible all the way to the tip of the lake, where this route ends. From here the Kibbie Ridge Trail continues down-canyon, and a cutoff leads eastward to the Horse Meadow Trail.

MAIN TRAIL #3

Deer Lake Trail: Crabtree Camp to Buck Lakes (Trail 20E16)

(Roadend: Turn east from State Highway 108 one mile east of Cold Springs onto Crabtree Road 4N26 and follow it to the Crabtree Camp parking area beside Bell Creek.)

Leaving the moderately forested red-fir and lodgepole flats of Crabtree Camp, we hop Bell Creek, making sure our canteens are full for the waterless climb to Camp Lake, and quickly come to a junction with the Chewing Gum Lake Trail on a sandy bench. Our route ascends dustily through open mixed conifers, then contours south, undulating gently, to reach a segment of older trail. We now assault a steep, much-abused path, fortunately well-shaded, which levels out under aspen and lodgepole at the junction with a lateral to Pine Valley. Open stands of mature Jeffrey pine, red fir and Sierra juniper allow a viewful traverse above deeply forested Pine Valley; then the trees close in as we track a red-fir corridor around a grassy pond and gently ascend a herbaceous gully to the signed Emigrant Wilderness boundary. One-hundred yards farther is the west end of shallow, green Camp Lake. This sparsely forested, sorely trampled small lake supports a harried population of brook trout. Campsites are found as we climb rockily around the south shore, and at the east end as well.

Across a saddle just past Camp Lake, we leave behind a spur trail to Bear Lake and a dank pond, and switchback down on deep sand flanked by dense manzanita and ceanothus to an easy ford of Lily Creek. Swinging southeast through a meadow sporting corn lilies, lungwort and groundsel, our path soon comes to a granite headwall, and makes a steep, rocky ascent. Now above most of the trees, we see, in the south, Pine Valley and the chaos of white domes in the Chain Lakes region. A parade of switchbacks leads to a lengthy traverse that passes through meadows south of black-streaked granite outcrops, and we soon reach a pretty lakelet, much larger than shown on the topo map, speckled with Indian pond lilies and backdropped by dancing aspens and lichen-dappled granite. Its clear, shallow waters support a thriving population of yellow-legged frogs.

After a short climb east of this tarn, we survey dome-guarded Toms Canyon in the northeast, Groundhog Meadow below in the southeast, and, on the eastern horizon, Bigelow Peak and the jutting prominence of Tower Peak. Bone-jarring dynamited switchbacks, esthetically ameliorated by a profusion of wildflowers in early season, lead down to a sidehill traverse in glacial boulders west of Piute Meadow. Keeping to the trees south of the willowed west arm of Piute Meadow, we pass a small campsite; then, where our route bends about to cross Piute Creek, there is another, larger site. Only yards after Piute Creek the Groundhog Meadow spur trail comes in from the south. The dry slabs and lodgepole pines demarcating the lower margin of Piute Meadow are left behind when our path bends upward on switchbacks, thrusting rockily up the east slope of Piute Creek Canyon to a broad saddle southwest of Piute Lake. Seen from this pass and from other points as we drop moderately down to the meadowed west end of Piute Lake are many rock-climbing possibilities. Good technical climbing on 400–500-foot-high faces of well-broken, aplite-diked granite is found all along the wall north of Piute Lake. The lake itself is small and grass-fringed, except where forested with lodgepole, and its shallow greenish waters support rainbow trout.

A fair campsite is on the lake's north shore, which we skirt before climbing gently and then dropping through lushly vegetated meadow to a ford of West Fork Cherry Creek, which can be wide in early summer. Interesting flowers seen in the jungle of flora preceding this crossing are the orange-and-maroon tiger lily, fragrant purple onion, palmate-leaved yellow cinquefoil, and stalked white rein orchis. East Flange Rock, a volcanic precipice to the north, and the upper reaches of Cherry Creek, including the technical dome, Peak 9002, swing into prominence as we climb along a steep, forested slope on switchbacks heading for Gem Lake. Heavy pack-animal use, inconsiderate short-cutting hikers, and water runoff have reduced the trail to a shambles of ruts and cobbles. We level out on a wooded saddle, then drop past two camps to the north shore of pretty Gem Lake, which sits on the edge of a glaciated granite bench. A thin strip of lodgepoles surrounds most of Gem Lake's rocky margin, and a striking wall of orange-rusted granite, offering good crack and chimney climbing, lies to the north. The best camping at this shallow lake is on the north shore, which our path parallels.

After passing an unmarked spur to the Wood Lake Trail, this route switchbacks up onto sunny glaciated slabs, speckled with sunflowers, pussy paws, buckwheat and stonecrop. An east-trending gully leads us to humus-bottomed Jewelry Lake, which is rapidly being meadowed in at its inlet. The gravels and shallow lagoons at the lake's head do, however, provide good spawning for the rainbow trout that live here. The dominant feature of the Jewelry Lake area, visible for miles around, is the 600-foot-high overhanging dome north of the lake, which would provide particularly challenging technical climbing.

Jewelry Lake

Tracking north of Jewelry Lake's swampy east end, we climb gently into sandy woodland where pussy paws and hairy lupine grow beside the trail. The path turns northeast for a moment, marking the best departure point for those making a cross-country visit to Wire Lakes, then back southeast to climb a slabby ravine shaded occasionally by mountain hemlocks. Atop the gully, the wooded outlet of Deer Lake is but a few strides ahead. Frequently the open north shore gives way to willow-choked meadow pockets and lodgepole groves. Proceeding on sandy loam around the north shore of Deer Lake, which has an ample fishery of rainbow trout, we pass a trail to Spring Meadow, then turn east through a muddy glade and past a dark, mosquito-breeding pond to a rock-hop ford of Long Lake creek and a junction with the Long Lake Trail. Zigzagging up through talus, slabs and pocket meadows, the path leaves Deer Lake behind, passes the Wood Lake lateral, and ascends moderately under mixed lodgepole and western white pine to a granitic gap. Then, descending east, our way leads past two early-season tarns which, with melt-off from snow drifts along the route, ensure June and July hikers an ample supply of mosquitos. We leap to the north side of a trickling creek that drains the steep canyon our path follows, dropping past huge talus blocks and a profusion of wildflowers.

At the Emigrant Lake Trail junction, we turn south along partly rockbound Upper Buck Lake. With a fine campsite at the southwest edge of its clear, 55-foot-deep blue waters, this lake has large (to 18″) rainbow trout and a 500-foot-high face above the wet meadow on the north shore. A sometimes tricky crossing of the creek draining Upper Buck Lake on the narrow granitic isthmus between it and the lower lake brings us to a

Deer Lake

Lower Buck Lake

camp in an idyllic lodgepole and mat manzanita stand, near an unfinished log cabin built by a now-defunct power company. We then traverse along the east side of Lower Buck Lake, which is entirely contained in shores of light granite. A stream-flow-maintenance dam impounds the trout-abundant waters, and is responsible for the few burnished silver snags which stand reflected in the yellow early-morning light. Among the living trees, lodgepoles and nodding-spired mountain hemlocks obtain tenuous footholds on steep-sided islands that break the lake's surface. Our path is usually covered with duff, under groves of hemlock or lodgepole, but occasionally we tread on polished slabs. Mallard ducks, gulls and plovers are often seen, as well as violet-green swallows. From Lower Buck Lake's south margin we undulate over broken granite and sand past two pinhead tarns to a signed saddle where we intersect the Pine Valley Trail (Main Trail #2).

MAIN TRAIL #4

Burst Rock Trail: Gianelli Cabin to Deer Lake (Trail 20E14)

(**Roadend:** Road 4N26, signed as the Crabtree Road, leaves State Highway 108 one mile east of Cold Springs. Follow this good dirt road past the turnoff to Crabtree Camp to the roadend at Gianelli Cabin, where parking is ample.)

The Gianelli Cabin trailhead stands in a much-abused 8560-foot-high meadow amid moderate-to-dense lodgepole pines and a smattering of mountain hemlocks and red firs. Our trek begins just across a miniature upper branch of Bell Creek, where we find what now remains of Gianelli's cabin — four tiers of lodgepole logs in a 15-foot square. As we "lower our gears" for the predominantly steep 600-foot ascent to come, we note that, unfortunately, even though our route lies on a boulder-strewn slope heavily clothed in timber, 4-wheel-drive and dirt-bike owners can also adjust their machine's gearing to cope with the grueling ascent. They have blazed two breakneck "trails," both cut deeply into the rich duff earth, which obscure or render useless the hiker's path. Not inclined to further the wanton destruction of this pristine terrain, we stick to one of these routes, and emerge, panting, on the sandy, pine-dotted plateau called Burst Rock, humbled but happy in the knowledge that the worst climb on Trail 20E14 is now behind.

Our level trail heads east under the high point of Burst Rock to the signed Emigrant Wilderness boundary, but lensmen will first climb that summit to capture vistas north across the deep gorge of South Fork Stanislaus River, where the large meadow that was once Gertrude Lake lies below. Volcanic mountains from Cooper Peak east to Leavitt Peak can be seen to advantage, while cerulean skies and lofty cumulonimbus clouds backdrop Tower Peak, the Saurian Crest, and Mount Lyell and the Clark Range far to the southeast. Burst Rock's name is a corruption of "Birth Rock," so called because a Mrs.

Wilson, member of an overland wagon train using the punishing Emigrant Pass trans-Sierra route, gave birth to a girl here, using a natural cave for protection from the elements.

The headwaters of Bell Creek are our next objective, and the trail leads east below the slabby summit ridge on gruss bordered by pinemat manzanita and mixed subalpine conifers. A shallow tarn's meadowed outlet stream is skirted before the descent ends at a viewful saddle where there is a junction with a short spur trail north to Powell Lake. This delightful granite-bound lakelet has two rock reefs extending into its shallow, humus-bottomed waters, which interrupt reflections of Cooper Peak and Castle Rock in the north and of mountain hemlocks fringing the lake. Nice but heavily used camps are nestled on the west and northeast shores. Fishing for small brookies (to 8″) is very good any time but midwinter, and the meadowed southern banks are great for fly casting.

Beyond the Powell Lake junction a dividing ridge causes the trail to ascend 300 feet, at first gently and then more steeply in an eroded ravine, before it levels out on the sandy ridge. Then, sidehilling down northeast, the path reaches a granitic outcrop from where excellent views encompass the entirety of Yosemite, Mount Lyell and Volunteer Peak being quite prominent, and the meandering path of Lily Creek below in Lake Valley, a boulder-pocked grassland in which Chewing Gum Lake lies. Thereafter our way becomes knee-jarringly steep for 200 feet on volcanic slopes cloaked in sagebrush and senecio, but we soon enough level out at the Chewing Gum Lake Trail. A party of California-bound gold-seekers was once trapped here in an autumn snow storm (it would seem that most Sierra crossings were ill-timed). They cut fire wood from lodgepole pines near this point — but 10 feet above the ground, indicating the snow pack's depth! Some of the truncated trees still stand.

Once again a volcanic-topped ridge stands in the way of our eastward progress, but, after we pass two grassy tarns and leave the lodgepole forest behind, the moderateness of the ascent leaves some energy for gazing at the *Pinecrest* north-country or pondering the difficulties one would have had 125 years ago, nursing a family and heirloom-laden wagons over this route. Atop the ridge, slopes of pussy paws and locoweed give way to mixed conifers, but still allow us to scan the southern horizon for the prominent glacier between Mounts Lyell and MacClure, or swing our gaze east and north to Tower and Leavitt peaks. Soft-spoken white-headed woodpeckers might also be seen, but more commonly the white pate will be possessed by the smaller white-crowned sparrow. Descending the northeast ridge of Peak 9201, we leave behind the views and the volcanic soil to switchback occasionally past pockets of green paintbrush, ovatum onion, lupine, buckwheat, miner's lettuce, and sulfur flower before striking the Y Meadow Lake Trail.

The next leg of the route leads over nearly level lodgepole-covered terrain on generally sandy, sometimes muddy trail to Whitesides Meadow. We swing near the South Fork Stanislaus River and a broken check dam which once held back enough

Castle Rock, Eagle Pass, Three Chimneys

water to completely inundate Whitesides Meadow. The Cooper Meadow Trail junction is reached when our route finishes rounding Whitesides Meadow's south side.

A short distance later is the Relief Valley cutoff, and just yards later we top the Lily Creek-Cherry Creek divide in a willow patch that snuggles against light granite bosses. Dropping steeply, then more moderately, we emerge from lodgepole forest to bisect a summer-dry volcanic meadow inhabited by pocket gophers and blackbirds. A few feet beyond this sloping flat is the Toejam Lake Trail, leaving due south. Uneventful walking in viewless lodgepole groves leads gently — though with a few short steep pitches — down to level trail near our linkage with the Relief Valley Trail. Here we turn south and arc down through bouldery forest to the banks of West Fork Cherry Creek in Salt Lick Meadow. The water here runs 20 feet side in spring run-off, but poses less difficulty later on. Across the stream, we track beside the old trail rut, which is cut deeper each year by running water and offers mute argument for the re-routing of all trails around fragile areas.

Climbing away from Salt Lick Meadow, a southward-bearing, steep, rocky-dusty trail leads to a crossing and then a quick recrossing of an early-season creek, after which the angle of ascent lessens. Soon we wind levelly through a predominantly lodgepole forest speckled with grassy tarns and white boulders fringed by dwarf bilberry and cheerful-looking red heather. Later, one passes a good camp just before stepping onto the edge of Spring Meadow. True to its name, Spring Meadow is lush and wet, to the point of having a cluster of boggy ponds south of the trail. Cinquefoil, lupine and penstemon live on its verdant surface, while corn lily, meadow rue and spiraea grow along the fringes. The ford of Spring Creek is a sandy 12 feet in early season unless one is willing to follow its meandering banks for some distance. Across it, the trail ascends easily east through bouldered open timber, keeping near the stream, which offers catchable brookies. Our path begins to veer southeast from the creekside, but the trail for the next few hundred yards would seem to have been designed to do double duty as both creek bed and footpath, it is so muddy and eroded.

The remainder of the ascent to the signed Wire Lakes Trail isn't much better, but we do have as many as four ruts to choose from in places! Later, beyond a pocket meadow, we pass a cairn-marked trail that leads east to Long Lake's north end. Soon after, we climb over a pine-timbered saddle, where red-breasted nuthatches and Williamson's sapsuckers are often seen, then drop to a willow-thicketed glade, foretaste of a delightful descent through meadows and past tarns to Deer Lake. Late in the afternoon, these ponds' surfaces become glassy-still, reflecting lodgepole snags and rose-hued granite boulders. The lowest tarn of the group, rimmed by red heather, dwarf bilberry and bog kalmia, is actually a nicer camping spot than any of the larger, named lakes in this vicinity. From it, the path leads gently-to-moderately down-canyon, crossing the unnamed creek twice before leveling out in sandy lodgepole flats north of Deer Lake. Then we cross the creek once more before striking the Deer Lake Trail (Main Trail #3) beside a damp meadow.

MAIN TRAIL #5

Cooper Meadow Trail: Coyote Meadow Roadend to Whitesides Meadow (Trail 20E15)

(Roadend: Turn east from State Highway 108 2.3 miles north of Strawberry, onto paved Herring Creek Road 4N12. It winds 6.8 miles, leaving its pavement en route, to a junction with the loop portion of 4N12. We turn right [east] and go another 4.9 miles to 4N12B, which branches south 0.8 mile to the Coyote Meadows roadend. Avoid parking spaces reserved for the Cooper Meadow cattle grazing permittee.)

The trail from the red-fir-forested roadend is not well marked. From the short spur road designated for use by the special-use permittee (cattle grazing), we climb a few feet east into a verdant but trampled corn-lily-and-willow meadow, where any of a number of bifurcating trails soon coalesce into a trail-jeeptrack which climbs steeply southeast, returning to very dusty trail under red-fir cover. Atop Cooper Peak's southwest ridge we find the Emigrant Wilderness boundary and a stock-drift fence. (Close the gate.) A short way beyond, Sanguinetti Spring, with its diverse floral accompaniment of aster, rein orchis, mimulus, ligusticum, cow parsnip, lupine, mule ears and others, emerges from the hillside a few feet above our gently descending path. Our wide track leads out of dark red-fir groves onto a volcanic slope mantled with lupine, scattered lodgepoles, and the bizarre-looking stalks of occasional green gentian. Above, turreted parapets of welded Pliocene pyroclastic rocks draw our eyes skyward. Shrill whistles, warning calls of the yellow-bellied marmot, punctuate the silence as we tromp northeast along the north side of Horse and Cow Meadow. Sweeping perspectives are had from here, from the spirey Three Chimneys to the east, south to precipitous Burst Rock, where pioneering wagoneers once rode. Much of Horse and Cow Meadow, which is used as grazing land by the Sanguinetti Cattle Company, is really dusty sagebrush flats, but a few pockets of true meadow are found before we leave its east end to plunge steeply down toward Cooper Meadow.

The frequently bifurcating trail, showing ample evidences of its use as a stock driveway, forces the conscientious hiker to make his own switchbacks, so as to do the least damage to the terrain — and to his knees. Most of the descent is under lodgepoles, but the remainder of the hillside, on up to cubic Castle Rock, is draped solely in a velveteen of sagebrush and mule ears. About 400 vertical feet below Horse and Cow Meadow, just after crossing the miniscule stream that drains Castle Rock's south flanks, we intersect a side trail to the Sanguinetti's range cabins which is the start of a cross-country hike down the South Fork Stanislaus River (Cross Country Route #3). Here we angle south of east for only a short distance along a

Trail Descriptions

fence line that bounds a horse pasture to the signed Eagle Pass Trail, in a dusty sagebrush flat. To continue to Whitesides Meadow, we turn south, following the barbed wire across sedge-and-penstemon-covered Cooper Meadow, noting eminently photographable scenes of quietly grazing stallions, or, over one's shoulder, of the ruddy, sky-scraping form of Three Chimneys. Leaving the meadow, an ascent on cobbly trail in a veritable forest of herbaceous and perennial undergrowth — gooseberry, mountain ash, willow, lupine, aster, Queen Anne's-lace, groundsel, mimulus, paintbrush and elephant heads — brings us to a saddle, from which we can gaze at the emerald expanse of Cooper Meadow and the South Fork/Middle Fork Stanislaus River divide as we pause for breath.

Next is Hay Meadow, reached by a gentle descent past a 10 x 20-foot log barn, built early in the second half of the last century by the Cooper for whom Cooper Meadow and peak are named. At one time, he pastured milking cows in these lush meadows, hauling the dairy products all the way out to the lucrative Sonora boomtown market! The wet meadow now supports only a battalion of blackbirds, emitting their harsh clicks as they forage for insects among the lupine and groundsel. Switchbacks lead rockily south from Hay Meadow, ascending a bouldery ravine to another, smaller meadow, this one surrounded by lupine, sagebrush and scarlet gilia growing on dark granitic rock. We skirt this meadow to climb a sedge-lined gully. At 8900 feet we emerge on a promontory just below the level of the overlying volcanic rocks, where, amid a handful of pines, one can see down the wide trough of the South Fork Stanislaus River almost to Pinecrest Lake. Here the route turns southeast to contour, with some undulations, over shrublands of sagebrush and lupine, typical of Sierran volcanic terrain, just below some weirdly shaped pinnacles and bluffs of auto-brecciated volcanic rock. Beyond a saddle the route gently descends through a grove of conifers to the slopes that border Whitesides Meadow. After crossing the wide incision cut in the soft alluvium of this pasture by the infant Stanislaus River, we amble northeast across anemic Whitesides Meadow, its lumpy texture caused by the excavations of pocket gophers. At the east end of the meadow, we meet the signed Burst Rock Trail (Main Trail #4).

MAIN TRAIL #6

Relief Valley Trail: Lunch Meadow Trail to Deer Lake Trail (Trail 20E12)

(**Roadend:** For access to the Relief Valley Trail, see the *Tower Peak* High Sierra Hiking Guide, Main Trail #1. It is about 6.5 miles from Kennedy Meadow to the Relief Valley Trail via this route.)

At 7600 feet, in a shady forest of red fir and lodgepole, the signed Relief Valley Trail leaves the Kennedy Meadow/Lunch Meadow Trail just beyond a trickling creek that emerges to cross our path from a thicket of alder, meadow rue, paintbrush and columbine. Our route quickly switchbacks up and over a domed nose, then parallels the dome's south face on a gentle northwest descent to a wading ford of Summit Creek. (The 40-foot crossing can be negotiated on boulders late in the summer.) On the far bank, amid shading lodgepoles, are two campsites just north of the trail. Abruptly, we climb out of the trees on sandy, rocky trail lined with Indian hemp and huckleberry oak to traverse steeply above the roiling gorge of Summit Creek. Buttress-rooted Sierra junipers give little shade on this slope, but we soon enough level out beside the now-less-raucous stream under aspens and lodgepoles, affording more shelter as well as nice camping. As we trudge away from Summit Creek, working south, then west, on deep sandy trail, there are infrequent glimpses of the precipitous southwest face of Relief Peak's west ridge, above Saucer Meadow to the east.

Meeting the old trail alignment, we swing southwest around a decomposing outcrop of light intrusive rock to Lower Relief

Valley. Here the stupendous volcanic prominence of East Flange Rock comes into view, dominating the western skyline as it did for pioneer parties in gold-rush days. After traversing along the overgrown meadow's north fringe, we turn across it, noting a sign indicating a nonexistent trail to the Silver Mine Creek Road (there is, however, a good cross-country route), as well as colorful sunflowers, buckwheat and pussy paws. Only a few trees protect us as we leave a campsite beside Relief Creek for a steep, dusty ascent on poorly maintained trail, bearing southwest under East Flange Rock's brooding face. This manure-strewn route has some of the few trail sections classified as "very steep" that will be encountered in the *Pinecrest* quad.

The angle presently abates to make a switchback down to a fir-canopied hop of Relief Creek, but not before we pause to examine a sand plate and wheel rim from one of the Duckwall Party's prairie schooners, which was abandoned here in late

Granite Dome, Lower Relief Valley

1853. These artifacts are nailed to a granite boulder beside the trail. We skirt a large camping area across Relief Creek, then climb steeply to another simple ford, passing more campsites en route. A final section of steep volcanic tread leads through lush vegetation, scattered hemlocks and lodgepoles, and possibly a lingering snowbank to finish the ascent in a sandy flat that has seen heavy camping use. Here, those whose angling urge dictates a visit to North (lower) Relief Lake should strike east to Relief Creek, where fishing is fair for brook trout to 12", then drop gently along its grassy banks, crossing to the lake when opposite it. North Relief Lake, where anglers will fare much the same as in Relief Creek, is a much more hospitable place to be based than its southern counterpart, owing to its more rocky surroundings which inhibits wind and mosquitos. From the entrance to Upper Relief Valley, the path stays along the west side of a lush meadow. Shallow South Relief Lake, lying in a meadowed depression, is easily reached from any point on this pleasant walk. A short distance later we meet the well-marked linkage with Trail 20E13, bound for Whitesides Meadow. This 1.2 mile lateral, a time-saver for those bound for the western Emigrant Basin, climbs gently up, southwest, through meadowed lodgepoles to gain viewful sagebrush- and mule-ears-clad volcanic slopes. A contouring traverse soon ends in a short descent on rather eroded tread to the well-signed Deer Lake Trail junction.

We proceed south on 20E12 across the now-sandy meadow, the lodgepoles on each side of which frame vistas of East Flange Rock and Night Cap Peak to the north, to cross Relief Creek one last time. After winding around tiny tarns strewn amid stunted lodgepoles and crystalline boulders which mark the Stanislaus-Tuolumne divide, we track south, descending gently into deeper lodgepole forest floored with a meadowy consortium of red heather, twinberry and alpine manzanita. The signed Deer Lake Trail (Main Trail #3) is reached shortly after the path switchbacks twice and levels out under immature conifers.

LATERAL TRAIL #1

Kibbie Lake Trail

Large, rock-girdled Kibbie Lake, named for Tuolumne County pioneer H. G. Kibbe, is the terminus of this pleasant trail, and a possible spot to spend the first night for those entering the Emigrant Basin via Kibbie Ridge.

The well-marked Kibbie Lake Trail junction, 5½ miles up Main Trail #1, stands in a fine duff-floored conifer grove harboring a small, grass-choked pond which lies just off the path to the left. Skirting this tarn, we near a ridgetop open space dominated by silver-haired dwarf lupine, pretty-face, used by the Miwok Indians for food, shield-leaved streptanthus, and buckwheat. This area is an ancient glacial erosion surface, as can be seen from the smooth rock surfaces and large erratic boulders scattered about. Presently our route enters Yosemite National Park and drops on rocky tread surrounded by chaparral, lightly treed with Jeffrey pines, into a small canyon. We amble north through sodden bottom land, passing the first lodgepole pines of our trip, which here, accompanied by white fir, form a dense canopy. Indian-hemp, false Solomon's seal, bracken fern, Queen Anne's-lace, violets, shooting stars and the delicate but deadly blooms of bleeding heart nod in the shadows, enticing the traveler to linger in coolness. But mosquitos, far and away the most numerous inhabitant of damp early-season forests, will no doubt urge you on!

The trail leaves the forest, climbing northeast onto granite slabs mottled by huckleberry oak, to a 6500-foot-high saddle. An observant naturalist will possibly encounter white, greenish-spotted explorer's gentian, discovered by John Newberry, physician for the transcontinental railroad surveys in the 1850's. The rocky route here descends to cross a tributary of Kibbie Creek under a south-facing dome which offers good rock climbing on its peeling skin. After the step-across ford, we closely parallel smooth green pools on Kibbie Creek, which is shaded by western azalea, willows and tall conifers. We pass a good camp on the right, then, just yards later, before a poorer trail climbs up amid huckleberry oak to the right of a granitic outcrop to continue over slabs to the west shore of Kibbie Lake, our route angles down to a 30-foot rock-hop of Kibbie Creek. A very good meadowed camp is found across the ford amid lodgepoles, before we turn up the creek over blasted granite ledges, our way copiously indicated by ducks.

Passing ice-scoured lagoons presaging Kibbie Lake, we reach its south shore, where camps are found in a lodgepole-and-labrador-tea fringe. Kibbie Lake, the largest natural water body in *Pinecrest*, is bounded on the west by gently sloping granite, while the east shore, which was on the Kibbie Creek glacier's downstream side, is characterized by steep, broken bluffs and polished bosses. Cross-country travel around the east shore is almost impossible, but you could continue along

North Arm of Kibbie Lake

the faint, ducked path around the west margin through lodgepole forest to reach impressive rock-climbing possibilities at the lake's north end. The waters themselves are shallow, with an algae-coated sandy bottom, where distinctively orange-colored California newts may take your bait if a rainbow trout (to 12″) doesn't.

LATERAL TRAIL #2

North Fork Cherry Creek Trail (Trail 20E94)

The North Fork Trail, now fallen into disuse, still provides a quick, scenic way from Lord Meadow to Cow Meadow Lake, as well as access to Yellowhammer Lake.

The North Fork Cherry Creek Trail has its vague beginnings in a sand flat, bordered on the east by granite slabs, about 150 feet north of the crossing of East Fork Cherry Creek in Lord Meadow (see Main Trail #1). Here, where the East Fork Trail can be seen to head east, following ducks, our route begins to curve north, then northwest, along the margin of a bracken-floored lodgepole stand to our left, while skirting a 40-foot rock wall to our right. Following ducks, we ascend gently along this outcrop, pass through a litter of downed lodgepoles, and emerge beside a wide, emerald-green pool in the otherwise roaring North Fork Cherry Creek. One might see a mallard duck, a summer transient, and its clutch of marbled ducklings dabbling here. A red-fir grove here, with sandy underfooting, provides restful shelter, but the through traveler walks behind the trees to ascend gently to a cliff-guarded defile before returning to the stream's east bank. A few hundred yards later we spot a blazed lodgepole bending over the far shore, marking our route's crossing. This ford could be chest-deep and very swift in high water, magnifying the poor footing provided by slippery boulders, so it should be treated with proper respect. Later in July it's a cake walk.

After toweling dry on sun-warmed slabs of light, aplite-diked intrusive rock, we ascend straight up the west bank of Cherry Creek for a bit, following ducks, to find the trail beside blazed Sierra junipers. We then turn to parallel the stream, staying on a forested bench below a tall cliff. Returning to the creekside from this essentially level traverse, the route peters out in a mature stand of red fir, so we stay near the slowly moving stream to find a ducked sand-and-slab route when we emerge from the trees. The next leg of our journey keeps us within 100 feet of the frothing white water, rarely presenting a true trail tread, but ducks are plentiful and the route obvious. Soon an incredibly blank unjointed friction face, 500 feet high, is seen on the North Fork's northwest wall, and we pass a fair camp. This marks the terminus of the Big Lake Trail (Lat-

At 7800' on North Fork Cherry Creek

eral Trail #3), which, in its last leg from Yellowhammer Lake, is a cross-country walk down the southern brink of a prominent gully extending east-northeast from the south ridge of Peak 8206. From below, this gully will be seen as the first possible way to go west from near the south base of the great friction wall. At the base of the wall, we turn behind a thick growth of young lodgepoles, eventually returning to our near-stream position in a wide-open slabby patch of huckleberry oak and lodgepole pine. A cascade at 7480 feet precedes more meadowy walking to come. At 7680 feet a 60-foot-high double waterfall is encountered, which we skirt to the left. Hikers proceeding down canyon won't have any trouble finding the way around, but those going northeast will want to begin ascending around the falls 100 yards below them.

Thin white petals of western serviceberry catch the eye as the forest opens up dramatically near the outlet of Cow Meadow Lake. Just in sight of the low stream-flow maintenance dam that impounds this lake, we pass a slightly garbagy packer camp, then hug the base of a 60-foot cliff along the western lake's north shore. (Cow Meadow Lake is in reality a series of lakes and marshes which, with the help of the check dam, run together in high water.) For this reason, the lake's size fluctuates widely, and, although its maximum depth is 36 feet, much of the lake doesn't attain more than a 3-foot depth. While the seasonal inundation of meadowland does kill many of the lodgepole pines that rim the shore, it also sweeps much food into the water, as well as providing good spawning areas, so Cow Meadow Lake's rainbow trout are big (to 15″) and numerous. Pleasant lodgepole forest is the site for many packer campsites as we wind north along the meadowed fringes of first Cow Meadow Lake, then North Fork Cherry Creek. Unfortunately, inconsiderate horsemen have marred the splendor with a plethora of cans and bottles. Soon we arrive at an intersection with the Pine Valley Trail (Main Trail #2) and the trail to Emigrant Lake, which is described in the High Sierra Hiking Guide to *Tower Peak*.

Author crossing Cherry Creek — 6′ deep and 48° — in late June near Cow Meadow Lake *Jeff Schaffer*

LATERAL TRAIL #3

Big Lake Trail (Trail 20E18)

Fishermen, sunbathers, lovers of austere high country and, especially, connoisseurs of solitude will value the ice-scoured area penetrated by this exciting lake-hopping route.

Trail Descriptions

The signed junction of the Big Lake Trail and Main Trail #2 is on the west bank of West Fork Cherry Creek in Louse Canyon. The first 150 feet of this route, dropping gently to the right along Cherry Creek was washed away by high water, and, although it is still passable, an easier way is found only 100 yards west, up the Pine Valley Trail, at the point where it begins to turn southwest, ascending gently through a lodgepole stand. Here our path breaks off due south and drops easily to a creekside sandbar overhung by tall lodgepoles and stately red firs. Numerous excellent campsites here line the chortling greenness of West Fork Cherry Creek as it passes banks of well-worn cobbles. As we leave the camp complex, sauntering easily over marbled slabs of varicolored mafic and intrusive rocks, Cherry Creek slides beside us, winding through a corridor of lodgepoles.

Then our track leads south, past another camp, to the high, cut banks of West Fork Cherry Creek. The 1-3-foot-deep, 20-foot-wide horse ford to sandy red-fir-and-lodgepole groves on the far side is out of the question for pedestrians, but there is a wading ford due east at the top of a sliding cascade. From here, scrambling south over fallen timber and another small branch of Cherry Creek, we reach the point at the foot of Louse Canyon's east wall where the trail begins a steep ascent, sometimes rudely switchbacked, over broken exfoliation shards. Cinquefoil, buckwheat and stonecrop grow at our feet, and a horizonward gaze encompasses a collection of unnamed domes down-canyon and the hulk of Granite Dome up-canyon. Still climbing, our way angles up the slope and through a granite notch 500 feet above Cherry Creek. A moment later we are on the west shore of small, wedge-shaped Rosasco Lake, which sits snugly in a granite cup, rimmed by lodgepoles and labrador tea. Biennial air drops maintain a fair rainbow-trout fishery here. Good camps are found just down from the outlet and on a spur trail at the forested east end.

From above Rosasco's southeast side, our eroded trail leads up to a divide, from where one can make out Haystack Peak

Big Lake *Jeff Schaffer*

and innumerable nearer domes in the east. Then, as we drop first steeply and then moderately southeast on poorly ducked, rotting slabs of dark schistose rock, we glimpse the high dome overlooking Jewelry Lake in the north. Levelling off on sand, we pass a signless junction with the Hyatt Lake Trail (Lateral Trail #4) and forty yards later, following blazes, cross a creek. Now our route becomes much harder to follow, but since the 250-foot ascent to Pingree Lake is over open slabs dotted with lodgepoles and some western white pines, we have no trouble heading for the small rivulet draining the saddle west of Pingree Lake, even if we lose the ducks. Following near the creek, we stay north of it and of the saddle's low point, crossing right under soaring granite domes which offer good rock climbing, and soon find the north shore of Pingree Lake. Belying its 54-foot depth, many sloping white islands, some graced by wind-stunted conifers, break the surface of Pingree Lake. A large packer camp is passed as we traverse the north shore, and less "civilized" sites dot the forest when we turn south. Secluded islands, meccas for the sunbather, could also be camped at if waded to. At some point along this shore, the tread will disappear, leaving you to walk gently over mats of red heather and climb east to a granite ridge where awesome vistas of the desolate southern Emigrant Basin and northern Yosemite present themselves. Tower, Kibbie and Haystack peaks are all easily identified, and Mt. Clark, in the range of that name south of Tuolumne Meadows in the southeast, shows ample reason for its original appellation — "The Obelisk." Mercur Peak, Gillette Mountain, and many of the other naked monolithic knobs so characteristic of this locality are seen in the south, across the immense, wind-torn expanse of Big Lake.

Our alpine romp continues southeast, easily negotiating open slabs to reach a glaringly polished, dome-bounded granite trough, where we follow an orange-stained creek sliding merrily south to Big Lake. Before undertaking this 400-foot descent you might consider going up the canyon to Kole Lake, an isolated alpine gem ideally suited for a base camp. Aptly named Big Lake (90 acres; over 100 feet deep) supports some hard-to-catch rainbows and has few good campsites, but the spectacular scenery invites a prolonged stay.

The next lake on our itinerary, Yellowhammer Lake, is a fine spot to base some explorations. We reach it by bearing southeast along a ducked path from a crossing of Big Lake's inlet stream where it turns west. A pleasant stroll leads to a granite rib, which we ascend, to be presented with two choices. First, if you want to stay at narrow, rock-girdled Yellowhammer Lake, you can drop gently southeast to that lake's outlet. Second, you can follow ducks northeast along this ridge through a dome-bounded gap, and then descend into lodgepole forest along the outlet creek of Five-Acre and Leighton Lakes, where you will find Camp Yellowhammer. Owned by Fred Leighton, constructor of the stream-flow-maintenance dams found throughout the Emigrant Wilderness, it consists of seven buildings and a corral, all made of logs hand-hewn from nearby trees. One could proceed from this point to Five-Acre Lake without difficulty. Yellowhammer Lake itself lies jammed between parallel granite bosses, which narrow its profile and limit camping to sites well away from the shore or, better, beside the small lake past its outlet. The 50-foot-deep waters must invigorate its inhabitants, rainbow trout. To reach the North Fork Cherry Creek Trail from Yellowhammer Lake, head for the prominent ramp leading a bit north of east up to the ridge south of Peak 8206, which can be seen as the large dome with a technically difficult southwest face.

Atop the narrow rib, we look east at North Fork Cherry Creek, flowing below in a textbook example of a joint-controlled stream bed. In the northeast can be seen a tremendous friction face on the north canyon wall. Our route of descent is a tight, huckleberry-oak-filled joint gully, whose south lip we follow until we can easily veer straight down the slabs to find the vague but well-ducked trail along the cascades of North Fork Cherry Creek (Lateral Trail #2). Hikers headed southwest will see this gully as the obvious line of attack just down-canyon from the massive unjointed friction face.

LATERAL TRAIL #4

Hyatt Lake Trail (Trail 20E29)

To sample the alpine epicure's austere delights, this spectacular lateral leaves south-southwest from the Big Lake Trail (Lateral Trail #3) about 40 yards west of the unnamed creek's ford in the glacially scoured valley separating Rosasco and Pingree lakes. Here a faint path proceeds down-canyon along an incipient creek. We keep close to the stream through meadow and forest, soon emerging onto water-oranged slabs on the lip of a barren cirque headwall. Stupendous vistas are had down this canyon to Kibbie Ridge and Cherry Creek Canyon, and we note the obvious cross-country route south past a 7100-foot-high grove of lodgepoles to Cherry Creek. From our 7780-foot overlook, the Hyatt Lake route follows ducks southwest, climbing slightly on the southern flanks of a slick dome. In a short time the ducks disappear, so we drop gently to the erratic- and conifer-littered saddle west of Hyatt Lake. This last half-mile exposes the hiker to steep friction slabs, and although most wilderness travelers will negotiate them with hands in pockets, the less experienced should take care.

Hyatt Lake lies but a few joyous minutes west of the 7660-foot saddle, in a glaringly polished granite wasteland relieved only by strings of erratics and occasional stunted lodgepoles. At the north end of this very deep (over 100 feet) expanse of shimmering water, deposited by incessant wave action, is a clean quartz-sand swimming beach, a Sierran rarity. Very good campsites are found adjoining this picturesque sandbar. Those who desire absolute solitude for angling (sporadic for large rainbows), sunbathing, brisk dips, or merely lazy introspection will chose a lone site halfway around the southeast shore, the best camp on this little-visited jewel. If one desires to reach Cherry Creek Canyon, however, one must backtrack to the opposite shore, which consists of a monolithic granite sheet buffed to an eye-piercing luster by countless applications of fine glacial flour. Here there are no high bluffs to bar access to Cherry Creek.

LATERAL TRAIL #5

Chewing Gum Lake Trail: Lake Valley to Crabtree Camp (Trail 19E21)

Winding from verdant Lake Valley past Chewing Gum Lake, a favorite of weekenders, then 1900 feet down through virgin timber to Crabtree Camp, this lateral, described from north to south, provides a fine finish for a loop trip emanating from Crabtree Roadend.

Starting at the 8730-foot-high dandelion-meadowed trail junction in beautiful upper Lake Valley, the Chewing Gum Lake Trail leaves the Burst Rock Trail (Main Trail #4) to wander over thick subalpine turf, with the precipitous north face of Peak 9040+, east of Bear Lake, as a guiding beacon. The route, sometimes without tread on the spongy green peat, passes south through a succession of pinched-off meadows; lodgepoles understoried by hairy lupine do the pinching. Then abruptly we veer west from this bearing, and climb slightly through a very wet meadow. Turning south again through a forested draw, we soon find ourselves standing on the shallow, grassy northwest arm of Chewing Gum Lake, beside which, in a fine lodgepole grove, is a very good camp complex.

Chewing Gum is a pleasant subalpine lake surrounded by porphyritic slabs which, due to weathering, prominently display their large feldspar crystals. The lake's 21-foot-deep, humus-bottomed waters' green highlights are augmented by willows, labrador tea, and lupine which crowd the shore, and these same shrubs offer camouflage for the brook-trout fly-caster.

A large feldspar crystal *Jeff Schaffer*

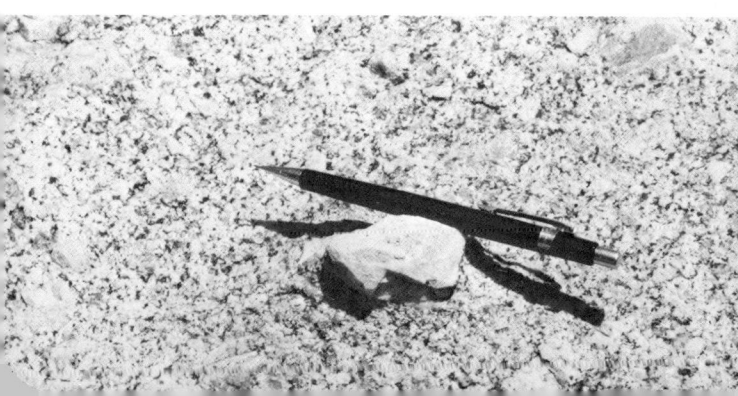

Chewing Gum Lake

Continuing south toward Crabtree Camp, we leave the west shore along an orange- and black-stained bluff, then cut south through a shrubby meadow where our path is momentarily lost. At the glen's south end we head 240° on the compass, following ducks steeply and rockily up to a level traverse in mixed conifers. Soon the trail deteriorates once again, as we descend a rotting gully amid myriad varieties of wildflowers. Aster, ocean spray, chokecherry, woolly sunflower and Queen Anne's-lace are but a few of the species seen. Leaving the gully, we cross a flat and then slabs, where there is no path save for ducks. While ascending southwest from these vague sections, avoid taking a ducked but hardly used route that drops steeply south to Bear Lake. Instead, make two switchbacks west into lodgepole-hemlock forest. Soon our climb switchbacks into red fir and western white pine, then makes a moderate side-hilling traverse which finally becomes steep, to the top of a bouldery morainal ridge with an open red-fir and western-white-pine cover.

After a pause for breath atop this 8980-foot rib, we begin the 1900-foot plunge to Crabtree Camp. This knee-jarring journey's first leg takes one moderately down through duff-floored red fir groves to a volcanic meadow that grows willows, corn lilies, Sitka valerian, paintbrush, lupine and senecio. Across this pasture we gently descend a sandy, less homogeneous forest to an 8340-foot nose. Here our path turns south and steeply descends a rocky gully to a seasonal stream running west between banks of cow parsnip, lavender mimulus, paintbrush, senecio and lupine. A well-shaded traverse keeps near the stream for one mile, and then we cross to another southward descent, this time through a tangle of huckleberry oak growing on dusty morainal till. Presently we re-enter red-fir forest, now more open, with some Jeffrey pines to reflect the lower altitude. This sandy segment leads moderately down to a signed junction with the Camp Lake Trail just ½ minute south of Crabtree Camp, across Bell Creek.

LATERAL TRAIL #6

Camp Lake Trail to Pine Valley (Trail 19E10)

This route, the first of four short laterals joining the Pine Valley and Deer Lake Trails, provides a good loop-trip linkage for trips begun at Bell Meadow.

Our signed junction on Main Trail #3 stands in a mixed grove of lodgepole, red fir, Jeffrey pine and aspen, with a littered floor of young aspens, larkspur, sweet cecily, senecio and yellow violets. Fifty paces south we emerge on the rim of Pine Valley's northern bluffs and are treated to a panorama, across its dark green expanse, of the jumble of white domes around Chain Lakes. Then we begin switchbacking moderately down over the treacherous "ball-bearing" volcanic hillside, where clumps of showy pentstemon, mariposa lilies and eriogonum relieve the drabness of this hot slope. Gradually, our way becomes more shaded under Jeffrey pine, aspen, black oak, and the rare combination of both white and red firs. Instead of making a junction atop the ridge dividing Bell and Lily creeks, as one might prefer, our route carves along the east slope of this ridge, descending moderately to reach the Pine Valley Trail (Main Trail #2) at 7050 feet. For the botanist, this route does have the compensation of many drought-tolerant wildflower types on display — stickseed, pussy paws, snowberry, phlox, campanulate onion, and mariposa lilies are but a few.

LATERAL TRAIL #7

Wood Lake to Deer Lake Trail (Trail 20E19)

From a trail junction near the outlet of Wood Lake on Main Trail #2, we follow east along the south bank of Buck Meadow Creek to a ford of that stream, which, in the first months of summer, is about 40 feet wide and 2 feet deep. Nonhorsemen will no doubt choose to continue to the massive many-hundred-log-jam that dams Wood Lake, then scramble up slabs to reach the trail as it works east atop a bluff. Skirting Wood Lake's north shore, our path passes its best campsite, on a forested promontory, and then another in a stand of lodgepoles, where we swerve north into a narrow gully. This rocky ascent soon levels off, and then our path drops to cross an intermittent creek. West of this stream, a few cobbly switchbacks take us moderately up a glacier-plucked step amid manzanita, ocean spray and phacelia. Next on the itinerary is a shallow subalpine tarn. Passing through the water-logged grassland north of its shores, you'll surely see dandelions and cinquefoil, and possibly a deer, a yellow-legged frog, or an aquatic garter snake. Three tiny tarns are passed, one of which sits astride the trail, before we reach the second mapped lakelet. Moments later we intersect the Deer Lake Trail, Main Trail #3, in a forested heap of morainal debris.

LATERAL TRAIL #8

Long Lake Trail (Trail 20E36)

Long Lake, one of the largest lakes in the *Pinecrest* area, is the destination of this half-mile spur trail. A signed junction with the Deer Lake Trail, Main Trail #3, is found beside the alluvial east bank of Long Lake creek, in the sodden meadows north of Deer Lake. Bearing northeast, we amble on sandy tread into a moderately timbered grove of lodgepole and western white pines, then, nearing Long Lake creek once again, the way becomes ducked to lead us onto a steep hillside of exfoliation sheeting. This ascent levels out about 50 feet below the 8700-foot lake level, winding among willows and boulders in a lodgepole-encroached subalpine meadow. The three short sections of concrete-and-stone check dam, built in 1939, are reached shortly thereafter. Long Lake is typically granite-bound, and dotted with numerous islands, some of which, if one is equipped with a raft for access, have trees and sandy nooks suitable for camping. Large packer camps are found on the north end, but most of the lake's margin is poorly suited to camping, being girdled by granitic bluffs with only enough level ground to accommodate a fringe of meadow or labrador tea, red heather and willows. From our vista point at Long Lake's impoundment, we see the bulk of Granite Dome looming up-canyon, as well as a fine rock-climbing face just east of the north shore. Sunbathing and diving are also attractions of this spot, as are hopes of capturing some of Long Lake's large rainbow trout.

LATERAL TRAIL #9

Boundary Lake Trail (Trail 20E11A)

The Boundary Lake Trail opens up the rugged splendor of northwest Yosemite National Park's Eleanor Creek country to exploration by the competent cross-country adventurer. Awesome rock cliffs, hewn by massive Ice Age glaciers, and numerous lakes, also the result of glacial action, are found in this lonely region, offering challenging rock-climbing, virginal fisheries, or weeks of wild solitude.

Spotted Fawn Lake *Thomas Winnett*

The unsigned Boundary Lake Trail begins on the Kibbie Ridge Trail (Main Trail #1) 0.6 mile east of Styx Pass, at 7320 feet on a steep broken slope of exfoliating granite. Just before one makes two small switchbacks and starts a traverse northwest down to Lord Meadow, a double-trunked silver-yellow lodgepole snag is seen south of the Kibbie Ridge Trail, marking the junction. A vaguely ducked switchbacking trail leads us steeply south toward Boundary Lake, presently becoming less steep through a jumble of lodgepoles and rocks to a forested tarn. From it, a final rise passes the limits of Yosemite National Park to a pair of seasonal ponds that connect with Boundary Lake's north side. Sandy flats softened by ovatum onion and sparse conifers make for good camping at this side of the lake; the east shore is composed of high bluffs. The trail around Boundary Lake's west side winds over granite outcrops, through patches of huckleberry oak and stands of fir and pine. Our undulating path keeps generally away from the irregular rocky shore, giving fair over-the-shoulder views north to Gillett Mountain's smooth south flanks, but sometimes we near the shore to find a snug camp in protective clumps of labrador tea or willows. Campers will find good fishing for rainbow trout.

At Boundary Lake's south end, we steer through a notched dome, then descend cobbly tread to a step-across ford of the outlet. On the south bank for a moment, we have telescoped views across the lake's slate-grey entirety before we turn south down a joint gully to the marshy north end of Little Bear Lake. Heading east of this islet-speckled expanse, we pass a fine packer camp on the north shore, then turn south behind a red-fir-and-lodgepole grove entangled in a marshy maze of brake fern and manzanita. At the south end of Little Bear Lake we have the option of descending south to granite-cupped Spotted Fawn Lake, which has camping in its north-shore lodgepole curtain. Spotted Fawn Lake, with its large rainbow trout, gives the adventuresome explorer access to the Inferno Lakes, Nance Peak, Edyth Lake, and the unnamed lakes of Kendrick Creek by rough but rewarding cross-country routes.

LATERAL TRAIL #10

Pinecrest Lakeshore Loop (Trail 18E10)

(Roadend: Pinecrest Lake is reached by paved road from Highway 108, past Summit Ranger Station (30 miles from Sonora) where Wilderness Permits are issued. Parking is available in large public lots across from the shopping complex. The northshore trail follows a dirt road past the public marina (at the extreme west end of Pinecrest Lake), while the south-shore trail is reached by walking east-southeast along the road through Pinecrest Picnic Area. At road's end, the trail takes over.)

The Pinecrest Lakeshore Trail, though a tame thoroughfare by wilderness standards, provides a nice afternoon for those with only enough time to sample the flavor of the *Pinecrest* country.

5621-foot-high Pinecrest Lake, a Pacific Gas and Electric Co. impoundment created in 1916, covers an old meadow and a smaller lake resting behind the terminal moraine of the glacier that once filled South Fork Stanislaus River's valley. This moraine is seen today as the sandy beach and hummocky terrain, dotted with grassy ponds, that bounds the southwest end of the lake. As the level of Pinecrest Lake drops (the water is used for power and irrigation in the Central Valley), the lake bed becomes a show-piece of glacial erosion as numerous glacially grooved *roches moutonees*, plucked surfaces, polish, chatter marks, spectacular erratics, and concentric recessional moraines emerge from the warm water. Also in evidence is the bouldery till smeared high along the south shore — a lateral moraine. Our path along the south shore starts in front of one of the many lake-front summer homes built here under Forest Service lease. Anyone may use the trail or beaches, but please respect this private property.

Proceeding levelly on packed-sand trail under windows and balconies in a classical Transition Zone forest of Jeffrey and sugar pine, incense-cedar, white fir, black oak and some aspen, we gradually leave behind the campground roar and most of its populace. The churn of motorboats, some trolling for rainbow, kokanee or brown trout to 15″, is soon forgotten as we concentrate on the surprising array of wildlife which tolerates the intruding hordes. Kingfishers, gulls, mallards, grebes, coots and

Pinecrest Lake from Pinecrest Peak Trail

mergansers are commonly seen on the water, while tanagers, robins, grosbeaks, juncos and, of course, the cocky Steller jay inhabit the forest's avian niches. Their mammalian counterparts are California ground squirrels, chickarees, flying squirrels and chipmunks. Larger mammals, seen only at night, are raccoons, porcupines, deer and an occasional wandering black bear.

Uneventfully rounding the south shore, we then, upon hitting the east shore, turn northwest over outcrops of gray-lichened granite and soon descend into a debris-strewn flat that was the Boy Scouts' Camp Bob MacBride. Only trash and broken concrete remain. Our route here turns northeast up a jeep trail beside a meadow of Queen Anne's-lace, brodiaea, saxifrage, farewell-to-spring, lotus, bistort and other middle-mountain flowers. A few yards brings one to a sign reading *Main Trail*, which marks our turning point north from the rocky track, which now becomes the South Fork Trail. Climbing slightly over rock, one soon finds the South Fork Stanislaus River, plunging, all afroth, through a narrow joint chute. Our way over it is eased by a sturdy bridge, letting us off on the north bank for a much rockier trip over broken slabs and under less-shady forest cover around the north shore of Pinecrest Lake.

Passing through another group of cabins, we meet a signed junction with the Catfish Lake/Pinecrest Peak Trail, then climb along steep granodiorite slopes, clothed in chinquapin, huckleberry and black oaks, above the dam. Past a quarry, we make a sandy switchback down to the concrete-faced dam's top, which is built of granitic boulders blasted from the canyon walls. Before this dam was built, an all-wood structure, built by a now-defunct power company supplying water to Sonora-area gold mines, stood near this site, impounding Edna Lake. In the meadows above Camp MacBride was another reservoir, called Eleanor Lake. At the dam's north end we find an unsigned trail to Strawberry, ½ mile west. Across the dam, our route becomes congruent with a rough dirt road leading south over the open ridge to a cluster of homes and the Pinecrest Marina.

LATERAL TRAIL #11

Pinecrest Peak Trail (Trail 18E09)

(**Roadend:** Follow directions as for Coyote Meadows Roadend but, after the right turn onto the 4N12 loop road (6.8 miles from Highway 108), follow Road 4N12 for only 2.7 more miles, to Road 5N31. Turn south on this road, to its end at 8025 feet atop Pinecrest Peak. Park off the road.)

Sampling varied terrain and vegetation, the Pinecrest Peak Trail is a good day hike for those who haven't time for longer trips or who have energetic children in tow. Downhill all the way, with lunch-stop possibilities at the unusual Catfish Lakes or at Herring Creek, this path is a pleasant introduction to the *Pinecrest* backcountry.

From our parking place 120 feet from the site of the Pinecrest Lookout, now nothing but a few broken concrete footings, we stroll down to that spot to take in sweeping vistas of the upper Stanislaus River drainage. Dodge Ridge Ski Area and a bit of Pinecrest Lake, our day's destination, are visible in the south, while distant Mokelumne, Dicks and Round Top peaks are seen on the northern horizon, above the Dardanelles. The Stanislaus River's deep cleft disappears in the smog-haze to the west.

Our little-used trail begins here, on the very lip of Pinecrest Peak, whose domed northwest rib provides up to 600 feet of rock climbing from easy scrambles to multiple 5.10 leads. From the lookout, our sandy path, indistinct at first but marked by ducks, contours gently down, south, through sparse mixed conifers. Mat manzanita and ocean spray are the dominant floor species, but others include stonecrop, penstemon, aster and spreading phlox. Juncos and raucous, gray, black and white Clark nutcrackers, named for William Clark of the famed transcontinental expedition, are the most oft-glimpsed avian species. Our route makes a couple of easy switchbacks down into a timber pocket, then levels off over a sandy nose, where the way is ducked and blazed south just under its east side. We lose almost 350 feet of altitude, then cross to the steeper west face of the ridge, viewing Pinecrest Lake, and drop down a rather bare hillside clothed in red fir and Jeffrey pine. At 7100 feet, within yards of each other, we pass the first specimens of black oak, white fir, and sugar pine, as well as further proof of our entrance into the Transition zone — bright blue Steller jays. Later, a dense white-fir stand is left behind for linked switchbacks down a steep spur choked with head-high manzanita, huckleberry oak and chinquapin. A shaded saddle ends the descent at 6710 feet.

Past the saddle's low point, we skirt a shallow, grassy, but nonetheless perennial pond which would furnish adequate camping, though the water should be purified, for rock climbers attempting challenging routes on the south face of Peak 6880+ to the west. A good overlook of Cleo's Bath in the South Fork canyon can be had from this gap. After contouring through second-growth white-fir forest around the north slope of Peak 6880+, we veer south, noting some spotted coral root, a saprophytic orchid which is rare in this area. In a dense grove of white fir, we ignore an old path heading straight, and instead take two switchbacks down to leveler terrain and where there's evidence of old logging operations: fallen logs, stumps and immature trees. The trail then goes west gently down to an unsigned junction with the Herring Creek spur, which leads to luxurious campsites beside Herring Creek, where small trout are easily caught. This junction, marked by an 18-foot-high erratic boulder and a large duck, stands in a beautiful grove of mature conifers only yards from the rush-shrouded east shore of North Catfish Lake. North Catfish Lake is a delight for the novice angler. Its shallow, grassy expanse, though choked with duckweed and other aquatic vegetation, is teeming with brown bullhead catfish. Though only 5-7" long, these fish, easily caught with a hook and 4 feet of line, can provide hours of excitement, especially for children. Catfish Lake, over a morainal hump to the southwest, is the same.

Turning south at the junction, our route winds around a muddy pond, its trees gutted by a thoughtless camper's untended fire. After a steep drop in a dark gully, the trail descends broken bluffs overgrown with huckleberry oak and black oaks. Levelling off, we turn southwest to traverse viewfully above Pinecrest Lake's north shore on a rock-and-sand trail which undulates in open terrain smelling strongly of kitkit-dizze, a pungent member of the rose family. Cobbly switchbacks soon lead down near the lake level, behind summer homes in a quiet forest. Passing between two of these houses — please respect this private property — we emerge beside Pinecrest Lake at the signed Pinecrest Lakeshore Loop Trail (Lateral Trail #15).

LATERAL TRAIL #12

Waterhouse Lake Trail (Trail 19E31)

(Roadend: Follow directions as for Coyote Meadows Roadend but, after the right turn on the 4N12 loop road 6.8 miles from Highway 108, follow Road 4N12 for only 2.7 more miles, to Road 5N31. Turn south on Road 5N31 for 0.7 mile, to a signed junction at a saddle. The road to the Waterhouse Lake Trail is the middle of three leaving south from this gap; the other two are signed as dead-end logging roads. Take this poor dirt road south through a meadow, where parking is ample, to the unsigned trailhead.)

Waterhouse Lake, easily reached in an hour's time, can be an overnight's destination by itself, or can be used to start the best day hike in the *Pinecrest* quadrangle — an exciting hike down the South Fork canyon to Pinecrest Lake.

Beginning at the Waterhouse Lake roadend, at 8100 feet among large red firs and some lodgepoles, our path skirts the exposed roots of a fallen fir to descend gently-to-moderately south to a senecio-speckled meadow. Circling the meadow, we step across a mapped branch of the Stanislaus River, then wind easily along another grassy swale, this one more lush. Turning from this meadow's edge, we pass under a dark canopy of red fir to the rocky rim of the South Fork's canyon, where one has comprehensive views of the upper reaches of that forest-bottomed trough. Here our route begins a scrambling descent south in a ducked gully. Ducks lead southwest out of the gully to broken slabs where the route is marked, at least for those returning from Waterhouse Lake, by stripes of luminescent yellow paint. Some of this slope is steep, but we soon level out north of Waterhouse Lake's outlet creek, which flows amid meadowy patches of lodgepole pines. Waterhouse Lake, 7425 feet, sits on a bench well removed from the Stanislaus River's path. To the north it is bounded by steep, shattered granodiorite overgrown with huckleberry oak, while its sandy south and west sides are flanked by lodgepole forests, in which good camps are situated. Much litter mars the bed of 17-acre Waterhouse Lake, but it won't detract from anglers' luck, for the lake supports good-sized rainbow trout.

LATERAL TRAIL #13

Eagle Pass Trail: Eagle Meadow to Cooper Meadow (Trail 20E08)

(Roadend: Turn east from State Highway 108 13.9 miles from Strawberry onto Road 5N01, signed for Eagle Meadow and Niagara Creek Campground. This road starts out poorly paved, but 0.4 mile later, when we turn south where Road 6N24 continues straight to Niagara Creek Campground, the road becomes well-graded dirt. Follow it to signed Eagle Meadow, where, south of Road 5N01, there is an unimproved campground with ample parking.)

Cutting straight across remnants of Pliocene volcanic deposits known collectively as the Mehrten Formation, the Eagle

Pass Trail treats hikers to geological enlightenment as well as spectacular subalpine scenery and expansive panoramas.

Our trailhead is found on the west side of Eagle Creek in Eagle Meadow, just across that stream from the hand-hewn buildings of Ospital's (formerly Martin's) Cow Camp. The path begins as a deep-sand jeep road south through the willows and clusters of lodgepoles in Eagle Meadow, which is fenced and gated (be sure to close the gate) to prevent the Ospital cattle herd from wandering. A pleasant traverse of the meadow brings one to the southern drift fence, then to Eagle Creek, which burbles over rounded volcanic cobbles of diverse coloration. A jeepers' camp is found beside this stream, which we hop across, leaving behind the tracks of all but the most dextrous vehicles. Here we earnestly begin a 1470-foot ascent to Eagle Pass, tracing a route up a hillside sea of tall herbaceous vegetation. Lupine, meadow rue, aster, penstemon, paintbrush, phacelia, farewell-to-spring, Queen Anne's-lace, corn lily, cow parsnip, scarlet gilia, mule ears, columbine, stickseed, and a host of other annuals thickly shroud the sparsely forested slopes. Across the creek in the west rises the precipitous east buttress of Eagle Peak, a 9385-foot tower of welded volcanic mudflows and alluvium. Because of many cliffs formed by more resistant rock, plus the overall friability of the material which composes it, climbing Eagle Peak would be a dangerous undertaking from this side, although much easier, at least to the base of the summit monolith, from the north or the west.

Our undulating but generally climbing path sticks to the eastern hillside, winding past occasional large Sierra junipers into lodgepole forests, sometimes meadowed, and groves of aspen. At 7900 feet, just after an open, steep stretch, the pines give way to red fir, through which we walk on deep duff past a good camp, to a ford of Eagle Creek. This ford could require removing your boots in early season, but later on one can keep dry hopping on large, stream-worn andesitic cobbles. Climbing steeply through a sloping meadow on Eagle Creek's southeast bank, we pass a signed but nonexistent trail to Bloomer Lake, then level off through open mixed conifers growing on dusty

Mariposa lilies

gray soil. After dipping to cross a small side creek, we begin a very steep section under red fir, mountain hemlock and western white pine. The path levels off for a moment at 8400 feet, only to resume its eroded ascent. One might startle a great horned owl in this quiet, bare-floored forest, or maybe sight a circling red-tailed hawk hunting the open areas.

The rough switchbacks abate at 8700 feet, soon after which we circle above another willowy expanse, this one growing on volcanic hardpan which, when wet from spring freshets or melting snowbanks, makes treacherous footing. A final steep pitch around the head of this meadow brings us to signed Eagle Pass, situated amid craggy volcanic boulders, and decorated with blossoms of red-tubular scarlet gilia and astoundingly bright yellow daisies. Vistas to the north are extensive. Looking past the ruddy knob of Eagle Peak, almost the whole Carson-Iceberg roadless area can be seen, and the high peaks of Desolation Wilderness, near Lake Tahoe, stand on the horizon.

Leaving this broad saddle, our route descends a cobbly slope clothed in sagebrush and mule ears down to a trickling rivulet in scattered pines. The rough trail continues south, soon presenting a view of Cooper Meadow below, and parallels and then crosses this stream, whose gorge is choked with an almost infinite variety of wildflowers in season. The rest of the hillside is a white velvet drapery of sagebrush, sprinkled with yellow mule ears and delicate clusters of mariposa lilies. Ending the 600-foot descent from Eagle Pass, we soon level out and find the signed Cooper Meadow Trail (Main Trail #5) at the north side of verdant Cooper Meadow.

LATERAL TRAIL #14

Y Meadow Lake Trail

A steeply descending cobbly ridge at the head of a volcanic meadow marks the well-indicated linkage of the Y Meadow

Lake Trail and the Burst Rock Trail (Main Trail #4). Our route leads a few feet south to a rib partitioning the Stanislaus and Tuolumne River drainages, then drops moderately to a gopher-roped meadow of dandelions, hairy lupines and tufted sedges. Winding southwest down this discontinuously meadowed canyon, which has exposures of marbled intrusive rocks where they're not obscured by volcanic alluvium, we soon glimpse Y Meadow Lake, then, past some adequate campsites, arrive at slabs demarcating its northern shore. The most desirable camp on artificial Y Meadow Lake, which is held back by an 18-foot rock-and-masonry dam, is found on the northwest shore in a pocket of conifers. Around the lake's east side, we note that the porphyritic quartz monzonite which here forms gentle slabs has taken on a rosy tint, quite picturesque in the low yellow light of late afternoon. Nodding-topped mountain hemlocks shade a smattering of sand flats along this shore, providing potential campsites.

LATERAL TRAIL #15

Bear Lake Trail

From the Bear Lake Trail junction on the saddle just east of Camp Lake on Main Trail #3, a well-beaten path skirts north of a large brown pond through shady lodgepoles. A short ascent over a sandy granitic knob brings us to a muddy stream at the south end of two meadows being encroached upon, in the normal pattern, by lodgepole pines. Ascending, we soon reach Lily Creek under high, broken slopes cloaked with huckleberry oak. Past a tepid pond, we sight the stream-flow maintenance dam impounding Bear Lake, and soon view this pretty but often overpopulated lake from camps beside its rocky outlet. The trail terminates a few yards later, at a large cluster of fire rings on Bear Lake's west shore.

LATERAL TRAIL #16

Toejam and Leopold Lakes

The unsigned Toejam Lake Trail is found a few feet after the Burst Rock Trail (Main Trail #4) leaves a gopher-roped meadow at about 8840 feet, east of Whitesides Meadow. The path can be seen to ascend gently south on sandy lodgepole duff. Soon it drops, with some steep sections, over a forested till slope to a small meadowed ravine. On a southwestward traverse in thick forest it soon reaches the final climb to Toejam Lake. On this climb we contour at about 250° along a hillside of rotting, varicolored granitic rock to a gulch which we ascend south. Ending in a pretty meadow that gives way to a sandy flat on Toejam Lake's north shore, this climb has good over-the-shoulder vistas north to East Flange Rock and Night Cap Peak. Toejam Lake is situated in a granitic bowl and rimmed with the typical subalpine combination of sedges, red heather, alpine manzanita and hairy lupine, with some senecio in the damper spots. While fishing for brookies in its shallow waters (20 feet) one has views northeast to Granite Dome. Very good, though exposed, campsites are found on Toejam's

Leopold Lake

west shore, near outcrops of schistose rock in sparse lodgepoles and occasional western white pines.

Heading south to Leopold Lake, a trip which should take some 20 minutes, we climb slightly through erratic-speckled sand flats colored by hairy lupine, huckleberry, sedges, onions and mixed conifers. Photographically induced halts to capture likenesses of the northern landscape, including the Cooper Peak-Three Chimneys divide, which shows up as a line of black crags against autumn snows, are well-rewarded. The north end of shallow, islanded Leopold Lake is reached in an open forest of lodgepole, mountain hemlock and western white pine. Mafic granitic rocks, tussocks of red heather, and bunched grasses edge its shoreline, which, though not affording exceptional camping possibilities, invites a stay because of the superb vistas across its wind-dimpled surface of Granite Dome, the Saurian Crest, and Bigelow, Tower and Forsythe peaks.

LATERAL TRAIL #17

Wire Lakes Trail (Trail 20E41)

The Wire Lakes Trail branches west from the Burst Rock Trail (Main Trail #4) in pleasant lodgepole-hemlock forest on the morainal ridge south of Post Corral Canyon. Climbing gently, the path leads north of a cluster of small mosquito tarns bordered by red heather and dwarf bilberry. After bending south, we pass over a bouldery ridge to find upper Wire Lake. Along its northwest shore, we see excellent campsites in meadowy turf. Upper Wire Lake has, like its sisters to the south, a good population of planted brook trout, which can usually be caught even if one's angling luck at nearby lakes has failed. Rounding peninsula-partitioned embayments and passing an excellent packer camp on the southwest end of upper Wire Lake, we turn south down the shallow outlet ravine to the rocky shores of Banana Lake, the middle Wire Lake. This shallow lakelet, having only one stand of hemlocks on its otherwise brushy and rocky margin, affords only poor camping, so one will most likely prefer to walk on to lower Wire Lake, just south of Banana Lake's midsection. Lower Wire Lake, most beautiful of the group, is set off from the granite basin in which it sits by a delicate rim of mixed conifers. Under the trees, bilberry, red and white heather, sedges, and delicate bud saxifrage form a thick rolling felt in the places where smooth granite outcrops don't rise from the cobalt-blue waters. Reflected in the lake are the high peaks forming the Emigrant Basin's northern boundary. The sum of lower Wire Lake's picturesque parts is a sublime alpine ambiance, and there are campsites to match along the east and south shores.

Upper Wire Lake

CROSS-COUNTRY ROUTE #1

Cherry Creek Canyon: Lord Meadow to Cherry Reservoir

Without a doubt the finest trek within the bounds of the *Pinecrest* quadrangle, the rugged traverse of Cherry Creek Canyon can be summed up in one word — granite. Granite boulders, slabs, talus and sand, spawned from soaring Yosemite-like cliffs and buttresses, broken from sensuously curving arches and exfoliating aprons, or ground by frothing whirlpools in spray-flecked, water-polished granite gorges — granite and its relatives make Cherry Creek Canyon the most exciting chasm north of Yosemite National Park. This route is not for the inexperienced, however. Frequent rock-scrambling and taxing route-finding problems make Cherry Creek Canyon a world accessible only to the mountain-wise explorer, and sometimes high water will hamper even the most resourceful of these. For safety and ease of travel, this hike should be undertaken only in good weather and when water is low, but the intrepid few who navigate Cherry Creek Canyon when the water is high and wild will be treated to an unforgettable experience. The rewards for all are total solitude, unclimbed domes and faces of Yosemite-like proportions, deep, clear swimming pools, virgin fisheries, and unspoiled forest camping. The hike is described here from Lord Meadow out to Cherry Reservoir; it is demanding enough without going uphill!

The start of our exciting trip through pristine Cherry Creek Canyon is found just after the last switchback into Lord Meadow from Styx Pass, at 7200 feet. Here we veer north from the Kibbie Ridge Trail (Main Trail #1) and traverse slabs and occasional shrubbery north to Cherry Creek, which is pooled wide and deep over green, sandy gravels. A short scramble brings us to the first of many precariously angled traverses on water-polished exfoliation slabs, 25-50 feet above white, cartwheeling cascades in the creek, which is more appropriately likened to a river during spring runoff. The cascades end at a small conifer grove, where there is a fair camp, and our rate of descent becomes negligible along the alternately pooling and rushing stream. Even here, where the flow is comparatively quiet, it would be impossible to cross Cherry Creek in high water, due to the depth and force.

Cherry Creek in upper part of cross-country route

Trail Descriptions

Turning just north of west, we begin a long ramble down sandy, water-worn slabs, sometimes climbing slightly to skirt thickets of huckleberry oak and bittercherry, under the brow of two spectacular multi-pitch rock towers, which loom from the north flanks of Mercur Peak. Near the influx of Yellowhammer Lake creek, the canyon floor is alive with plants — paintbrush, phlox, Bridges' pentsemon, serviceberry, pretty face, wallflower, hulsea and onion are among the notables. But later, as the 1000-foot-deep canyon bends north, the slick granite is devoid of life except for a few bonsai-like miniature lodgepoles managing an existence in seemingly sterile cracks.

Beyond the Big Lake stream, we re-enter a forest of sorts, finding Jeffrey pines beside willow-margined cataracts. Walking through sand flats where Cherry Creek Canyon begins to turn southwest, following the master-joint system which defines most northern Yosemite drainages, we pass a campsite while gazing all around — to Peaks 7890, 7431 and 7746, plus others — at the nearly unlimited rock-climbing possibilities presented on nearby granitic bluffs. Passing, at 6400 feet, into another slickened chute of exfoliation flakes, we note that our route along the water's edge is pinched off ahead, along even steeper slabs, so we climb south for 50 feet to round east of a low dome. Since our way back to the riverside would be thwarted by horrendous cliffs in a chute between two remarkably striated domes, both of technical difficulty, we stay high, scrambling through a tangle of huckleberry oak and mountain maple 100 feet up to the backside of the next ridge south. Expansive panoramas of the terrain down-canyon can be had by walking to the high point of this dome. Rattlesnakes make the shrubbery-dotted slabs atop this rock their home, so walk with care.

After descending this dome's sloping south side, we once again choose to remain away from the creek and the steep rocks that border it at 6000 feet. The sandy Jeffrey-pine-shaded flats on the east side of the next dome afford hospitable camping, if you decide to lay over. If not, saunter south,

then southwest, over lustrous glacial slabs to a large swimming hole where Cherry Creek momentarily eases its raucous descent. A fine campsite graces the sandy banks here, where hunched junipers and Jeffrey pines foreground a roiling potholed chute notched deeply in the monolithic granite. Highshooting torrents of white froth, enveloping the hiker in cooling, rainbow-generating spindrift, complete the scene, but to the through traveler, it means another detour. After a short thrash in herbaceous vegetation around a small dioritic dome, we rejoin the stream in a stand of conifers fragrant with the lilting aroma of white, yellow and rose-colored western azalea. For the next few minutes, we stay just under the 5600-foot level on rotting ledges of diorite cut by multitudes of lighter dikes, well above the cleft path of Cherry Creek, which has weathered oddly-shaped potholes in the surrounding rock.

Nearing the north shoulder of an impressive cliff, we follow a series of ledges that lead down to a sloping ramp covered with manzanita, to avoid any difficulties. Soon we find ourselves at the base of a fine waterfall in a rubble field that contains a broad spectrum of intrusive rock types. Fearsome (or inspirational, if one is a rock climber) views of the stupendous 700-foot dihedral-cut cliff to the east repeatedly draw our eyes from our footing as we scramble around a rocky nose east of the stream that drains a tiny lake on Cherry Ridge. Presently, a mature mixed-conifer forest closes around us at the most idyllic spot in the entire Cherry Creek Canyon, and possibly in *Pinecrest*. Here Cherry Creek runs up to 70 feet wide and 7 feet deep over foot-soothing sand and gravel, cutting 2-3 feet into the dark alluvium of this pristine lowland. Mammoth specimens of Jeffrey and sugar pine, incense-cedar and white fir, possibly of record proportions, shade a mattresslike pineneedle-strewn floor — a virginal site for a memorable camp. Bigleaf maple, flowering dogwood and rattlesnake plantain reflect the diffuse yellow light of the understory. Travelers

---

Left: Dome about halfway down Cherry Creek cross-country route

whose penchant for strenuous activity is not overcome by the delicious lethargy of this quiet locale will no doubt challenge the untrod technical precipices that loom over the camp. Truly confirmed masochists, however, will try the swimming.

All good things must end, as this restful forest soon does, giving way to rocky bluffs up which one must scramble, to traverse under some more technical faces which give the hiker feelings similar to those that the discoverers of Yosemite must have experienced. Near the east edge of a swimming hole complete with sand-bar beach, the rocks above close in, forcing us down a group of third-class but unexposed slabs and ledges to a little forest south of that pool. The only alternative to this tricky section is to cross Cherry Creek from the forest back around the bend, then recross just below the pool via two huge fallen trees. From this lagoon, it is best to remain near the stream, with some deviations to avoid bluffs, huge down logs, side creeks, and the odd morass, until you emerge from the forest at another, very deep, basin located ¼ mile below the influx of West Fork Cherry Creek. Turning south from the nice camp beside it, we traverse slabby granodioritic rock showing prominently, on the slopes to the south and east, red and orange weathering of iron from the rock's dark mafic minerals.

Once more our way is barred down the creek, forcing us to climb south on the crumbling slopes of a southwest-jutting rib, to find a poorly ducked path that leads down a gully on its lower side, then vanishes. Bulling our way through a thicketed forest of ponderosa pine and white fir, we soon regain Cherry Creek, in a section where it cascades through stepladder pools. Now descending east, we reach an unnamed creek coming down from Kibbie Ridge.

Hikers intent on reaching Cherry Lake should note that the way down-canyon to the reservoir's head is blocked by fourth-class slabs on Peak 5319, so one must follow the unnamed creek, or more open terrain to its south, 400 feet up to a saddle, mantled in manzanita and huckleberry oak, to the east of

Cherry Reservoir

that peak. Here the hiker has two options, depending on which masochistic tendencies he wishes to coddle. The first alternative is to continue climbing southeast through forested shrubbery to the Kibbie Ridge Trail somewhere in the vicinity of Shingle Spring, 700 feet above. Hobson's second choice is to climb south for only 250 feet or so, to the poorly defined ridge that slopes southwest to the east shore of Cherry Reservoir. Rather difficult cross-country hiking, over rough, rocky and brushy terrain, takes one down this ridge to a traverse of Cherry Lake about 100 feet above its cliffed shore. Numerous deer trails aid in this frequently frustrating trek, which presently finds a poor ducked route along the drab, barren shoreline. The large lake is nicely unpopulated, however, except by large trout, which are numerous. Eventually deposited right beside the water, we are forced to scramble awkwardly along its loose, dusty, till banks to a point opposite Cherry Lake's only island. Here we find some old logging tracks, and by sticking to the ones that are going our way, namely, along the shore, our travails are soon rewarded by a good road which emerges from the lake's seasonally fluctuating waters. A short distance along this brings us to the signed Kibbie Ridge Trail.

CROSS COUNTRY ROUTE #2

Karls, Leighton, Kole, Coyote and Red Can Lakes

The easiest route into the Karls Lake basin is via the Karls Lake Trail, which is found on the south shore of Wood Lake in a shallow ravine. From the signed junction the path steeply ascends sandy duff under a moderate pine cover to level off just west of a narrow col. As we begin to descend, the broad depression that holds Karls and Leighton lakes comes into view, while Bartlett Peak, on the Yosemite boundary, rides the southern horizon. The basin that stretches before our feet is constructed of highly glaciated slabs overlain by a thin green shroud of lodgepole pines, and where the glaciers' weight was enough to excavate the granite sufficiently, there now rest sparkling blue lakes, flecked with islands of resistant rock or of heaped till. Ducks mark our way steeply down intervening slabs to the meadow-floored lodgepole groves that hide the north shore of Karls Lake. Our trail rounds the west shore of this shallow basin, visiting a few good campsites en route. Rainbow trout find a home in the warm water, which beckons the trail-grimy hiker to bathe near shores lined with red heather and labrador tea. At the western extreme of Karls Lake, two cross-country routes depart.

Coyote Lake is easily reached from this point by walking west past two mosquito-spawning mud puddles, then angling northwest over slabs under a haughty 100-foot granite nose. Underused Coyote Lake sits west of this outcrop, in a dense lodgepole forest frequented by nutcrackers and finches. Its heather-rimmed waters, while a fine bivouac for transient mallard ducks, make a poor habitat for small brook trout.

Travelers with a sojourn to the west end of Leighton Lake or to Kole Lake in mind should, as on the route to Coyote Lake, proceed west past the second of two black ponds, but should then turn south and climb gently over rocky country softened by clumped sedges and club moss. Dropping through a low gap, you arrive at Leighton Lake's north shore, surrounded by silver snags and fallen lodgepoles, victims of its dammed waters. These dead trees, combined with the murkiness of the shallow water, the barren granitic islands, the infinite, hostile mosquitoes, and the general lifeless ambience of the environs, make this a place little-visited by hikers. Heading for Kole Lake from Leighton Lake's west end, we easily negotiate, at a 250° bearing, a slope of exfoliating granite. As we climb higher, photographers will be tantalized by unfolding vistas to the east. Atop the western saddle, our field of view encompasses all the peaks of the eastern Emigrant Wilderness, from those north of Lunch Meadow to Tower, Michie and Kendrick peaks inside Yosemite Park. Presently we arrive at the alpine-manzanita-clad shores of Kole Lake, a natural water body with a poor rainbow-trout fishery greatly outnumbered by yellow-legged frogs or, in the shoreline grasses, by easily disturbed hordes of bronze dragonflies.

Hikers intent on Five-Acre or Red Can Lake should, from the west banks of Karls Lake, proceed south to its outlet, where Leighton Lake's snag-littered shores are but a minute away. Rounding this lake's outcrop-bounded east end, we reach a meadowed gully that climbs east to a gap under the dappled shade of western white and lodgepole pines. A profusion of wildflowers enhances our descent north-of-east to a corn-lily meadow at the west end of Red Can Lake. Red Can Lake is mostly bound in granite, with frequent bluffs dropping to the deep water. Fine camps are found in a north-shore cluster of lodgepoles and on the sandy east shore. From perches in hemlock trees, chickadees, goldfinches and warblers provide tuneless ditties by which to gauge the silence, while the water's ferocious rainbow trout, to 12″ in length, provide other pleasures.

CROSS-COUNTRY ROUTE #3

South Fork Stanislaus River from Pinecrest Lake to Upper Relief Valley

This long route follows the sparkling South Fork Stanislaus River from Pinecrest Lake, at 5621 feet in the Transition Zone, all the way to its headwaters, at 9460 feet, at timberline on the border of the Hudsonian and Arctic-Alpine life zones. Hence this exciting trip, already diverse geologically, passes through four different life zones as well.

At the east end of Pinecrest Lake, we find the Cleo's Bath Trail, which guides us for the first leg of our journey along the South Fork Stanislaus River, in a meadowed glade of black oak and incense-cedar that used to be the site of the Boy Scouts of America's Camp Bob MacBride. All that remains of the camp are some stone fireplaces and broken foundations, and a jeep road climbing gently northeast through the forest. This road is now our trail, and we walk along it, ignoring a *Main Trail* sign which indicates the Pinecrest Lakeshore Loop Trail (Lateral Trail #10). As we continue gently up, with some short moderate pitches where the tread was ruthlessly blasted from the gray-lichened granodiorite, the forest peters out in favor of open slabs with manzanita, Jeffrey pine and some junipers scattered about. The bulging overhangs of grouped 700-foot rock faces to the north attract our eyes if we're rock climbers, while history buffs will note red-rusted scraps of riveted metal, cable and spikes beside the trail. These are remnants of steam-driven "donkey engines" which helped to build the dams that impounded water here for downstream gold-mining activities before the turn of the century.

Past the boiler of one of these engines, we emerge on a flat nose where the interested hiker can traverse at 300° to the remains of one of these dams, the lake behind which was called "Eleanor". We can clearly see the waterline of this reservoir preserved on the rocks and on old snags in the empty lake bed, now choked with willows and immature pines, all of which are cut off at the same height. From this rock rib we follow painted arrows down to the sagebrush-floored meadow. Traversing behind willows that all but prevent access to the South Fork, we wind levelly through fields of wildflowers. In a few minutes we come alongside the stream, then re-enter shrubbery at a sharp turn in the sand-cleft stream bed. A red-fir grove on the right provides good camping. Beyond it we walk on slabs above alder-lined banks to the abrupt talus-footed headwall that marks the end of our defined trail. Just past a spring-muddied tunnel in a high thicket where mountain kingsnakes, the almost-look-alikes for coral snakes, are sometimes seen, we find a duck marking the beginning of a scrambling ascent over mossy ledges and under the branches of gold-cup oaks to Cleo's Bath. The ducks lead us, panting, to a sand flat on the rib just above Cleo's Bath, where heavily littered campsites are found under some junipers and Jeffrey pines.

Cleo's Bath, a shallow, sand-bottomed, willow-lined pool situated below a series of sparkling cascades and whirlpools, is a favorite destination of weekend sun-worshippers. At times, upwards of thirty people can be seen broiling on nearby slabs or partaking of the brisk waters. The ducks we've been following end at the campsites, so we push on beside the rockbound river as it flows over sluiced rock plates or pauses to circle in deep green tubs. For the next 1/3 mile, while gazing at a succession of clean climbing walls across the canyon, we negotiate slippery exfoliation features, sometimes climbing well above the stream to avoid difficulties. At 6200 feet we come to First Forest, a pleasant mixture of white fir, cedar, and sugar and Jeffrey pines, plus an occasional black oak, cottonwood or aspen. Here it is advantageous to hop boulders to the Stanislaus' north side. The forest's thick duff floor has numerous good campsites to lunch at, before we push on, back to open slabs and a more raucous stream. Sparse junipers relieve the universal granitic grays with their sienna and olive hues, while cream-colored cinquefoil, white yarrow, red paintbrush, yel-

Trail Descriptions

low senecio, and the pink blossoms of farewell-to-spring brighten the landscape where soil permits.

Above a small series of falls we cross back to the south bank to traverse a slick exfoliation surface past house-sized erratics. Denizens of the foaming waters likely to be seen here are the drab brown water ouzel, a bird as at home under water as it is above, and yellow-legged frogs, who hide from the midday sun behind waterfall curtains. Entering Second Forest, a rare stand of mature mixed conifers, we pass an excellent camp beside the South Fork, which pools deeply beside banks of bracken and willow. We're forced to veer uphill momentarily, away from the Stanislaus, but soon return to traverse forest-floor litter and bracken to another series of open, step-laddered cascades. The cliffs to the north would provide climbs of from one to three pitches.

Nearing the influx, from the south, of a minor tributary, we traverse around huckleberry-oak thickets to avoid worse conditions at creekside. At this side stream (6720') we cross the South Fork once again and then climb moderately past beautifully water-sculptured, brown-patinated granite down which the Stanislaus leaps. Huckleberry oak, red-ossier dogwood, willow, shrubby spiraea, manzanita and bittercherry are the woody species that flank the stream as we near Third Forest, situated on the branch stream coming steeply down from the north. The way around the Stanislaus' north bank is made impassable by an under-aspen tangle of alders, so we're forced to ford once again, then traverse a thigh-high ground cover of fern, twinberry and thimbleberry to a good camp on the south bank. As soon as possible after passing Third Forest we recross the river.

Those who want to take the recommended detour to Waterhouse Lake should bear at about 35° from this crossing, breaking free from the vegetated canyon bottom to open slabs. Heading along the small, sliding creek that is Waterhouse Lake's drain, we climb easy slopes marked by bas-reliefed

---

Left: At 6200' on South Fork Stanislaus River

xenoliths, mouse-tailed ivesia and stunted junipers to the densely forested west shore of Waterhouse Lake. The best campsites around the lake are found here.

To resume our trek up the Stanislaus we skirt Waterhouse Lake's south shore, where more camps are found in sandy flats and forested nooks, then climb east from its inlet, avoiding aspens and mosquitoes by keeping above them to the south. Passing just north of Adele Lake, a dinky affair of interest only to the most rabid angler, we cut southeast over the shoulder of the knob to the south, soon topping out at an overlook amid lodgepoles. Sighting south over the huckleberry-oak scrub and slabs by which it is reached, we see an immense meadow of saw grass and willows which used to be Gertrude

Cooper's first cabin (built 1865) in Cooper Meadow

Lake. Like its sisters down-canyon, this reservoir was impounded by an all-wood dam, the remains of which can be seen at 7350 feet. Across the canyon we can see the cliffs on Burst Rock's north face.

Dropping down into the grassland, we turn east to wind through head-high jungles of cow parsnip, self-heal, Queen Anne's-lace and paintbrush to the Stanislaus, which bends north here. When possible, ford to its south bank, then wind over many fallen logs. Where the river turns south, ford again and keep almost 0.2 mile from the creekside to avoid entanglement in horrendous thickets of alder and willow. Soon the Horse and Cow Meadow tributary of the Stanislaus is crossed, and we climb east along a mafic ridge, well above the narrow, rock-choked gorge cut by the river. This hot traverse leads to a shrub-dominated meadow just under 8000 feet, where we branch northeast along the Stanislaus' Cooper Meadow fork. This stream canyon is conspicuously marked by boulders of brecciated volcanic material, heralding our ascent into the rocks of the Mehrten Formation which mantle the summit reaches of the Sierra.

Presently the climb levels out along a wide, deep stream that flows past colorful banks of Queen Anne's-lace, lupine, yarrow, mimulus, mariposa lily and mountain ash in a quiet lodgepole forest. Color is in the air, too, in the form of finches, warblers and juncoes. Castle Rock and the Three Chimneys swing into view, standing at the apexes of seemingly naked hillsides of more friable debris. A bifurcating cowpath leads us into Cooper Meadow, and, cutting across the grassland with its cinquefoil, pentsemon and little elephant's heads, we reach two cabins, owned by the Sanguinetti Cattle Company. These two buildings, the first built in 1865 and the "youngest" in 1875 by Mr. Cooper, for whom this meadow is named, have been used for cattle operations ever since. Unfortunately, the Forest Service, in a rash directive lacking in historical perspective, has decreed that these two cabins, beautiful examples of now-gone craftsmanship, be destroyed by 1985 so that the

Emigrant Wilderness will not be marred by the presence of man-made structures. Were these houses closer to civilization, they would no doubt be designated historical monuments, but in the rugged backcountry, which they reflect in every curve of their rough-hewn timbers, they are deemed undesirable! (On entering and leaving the corral surrounding these cabins, be sure to close the gate.) From the second gate we can follow either a wide path going northeast or the meadow's fence line, trending more eastward, to the trail from Coyote Meadows Roadend (Main Trail #5) and its junction with the Eagle Pass Trail.

Cooper Meadow, Three Chimneys, Sanguinetti Cow Camp

Trail Descriptions

To continue into Cooper Pocket and thence to Upper Relief Valley, we leave these trails behind and stroll east over the clumpy remains of Cooper Meadow and into a moderate forest. Easily leaping the infant Stanislaus, we trace an intermittent use trail through patches of meadow that have representatives of almost all herbaceous species found in the upper Canadian Zone. Above us, the Three Chimneys' south face looms forbiddingly, a study in reds and brown. At 8520 feet we pass a decrepit packer campsite in a grove of mountain hemlock. Leaving this dank spot, our route up the Cooper Pocket headwall leads along the north bank of a branch stream that curves south of volcanic Peak 9189. Our steep ascent under western white pine, hemlock and red fir passes a meadow at the 8800-foot level, them climbs in earnest toward the ridgetop in the southeast. Hemlock forest fades as we climb the clayish volcanic soil, pantingly gaining the ridge at 9460 feet. Here one wants to drink deeply of the clean, cool air and the exhilarating vistas of the volcanic peaks ringing the upper South Fork Stanislaus River. This ridgetop, right at timberline, bears stunted, wind-beaten lodgepole and white-bark pines that find a meager subsistence on the cobbly volcanic soil, while more ephemeral herbs soften the moonscape with pastel shades. Green gentian, dwarf lupine, mule ears, buckwheat, mouse-tailed ivesia and rockfringe are among the species that seasonally grace these slopes.

From this rest spot we contour southeast to a second arm of the ridge, from which verdant Upper Relief Valley and the Relief lakes are seen almost 700 feet below. Scrambling down on a treacherous volcanic hardpan, we angle southeast toward South Relief Lake. A much more diverse assortment of wildflowers is seen on this descent, which might be accomplished under the watchful eyes of a soaring red-tailed hawk or sparrow hawk. Bottoming out, we penetrate a shallow fringe of sagebrush and lodgepole before reaching the Relief Valley Trail (Main Trail #6) just west of South Relief Lake.

Climbers

UNLIKE THE TRUE HIGH SIERRA to the south, *Pinecrest* is not a country for mountaineers. No high, knife-edge arêtes or windswept, splintered pinnacles exist in this area to tempt those who desire that top-of-the-world exhilaration that mountain-climbing brings. In fact, few prominent peaks of any kind are found in *Pinecrest*. The great Ice Age was responsible for the Emigrant Basin's rolling character; its glaciers completely overrode the land, shearing away any sharp ridges and smoothing all the peaks. So ambitious mountaineers tend to shun *Pinecrest*, setting their sights farther south. Unfortunately, in doing so, people miss out on the best and largest rock-climbing area in the Sierra north of Yosemite, and the only almost unclimbed region in all of California. Throughout *Pinecrest*, 400- and 800-foot-high walls, slabby aprons, and domes abound, all boasting exceptionally clean rock untouched by rock climbers. Much of the climbing involves friction and exfoliation-flake cracks, but many faces also afford face-climbing and jam-cracks. In Cherry Creek Canyon and the South Fork Stanislaus River canyon above Pinecrest Lake, which are the two longest continuous areas with high-angle rock possibilities, one climbs among vertical walls that are streaked with black water stains and that have tall coniferous forests at their feet, much like Yosemite Valley but without its attendant crowds, noise, air pollution or scarred rock. Good access to the summits and bases of *Pinecrest*'s walls without rappelling makes it easy to climb more than one route in a day.

These precipitous climbs are not for the casual mountaineer. Special equipment is required for safety, but even more important is rigorous and extensive training in safe techniques. Those interested in learning to rock-climb should contact the Sierra Club or other mountaineering organizations for classes.

The steep volcanic summits on the north boundary of the Emigrant Wilderness in *Pinecrest*, should in general be avoided,

---

Left: Steve Weldon, Tuolumne County Search and Rescue, in rescue on Pinecrest Lookout Rock

because they are composed of poorly cemented volcanic debris that affords no anchoring points and will break apart almost without provocation.

To help rock climbers find interesting faces and spots for extended base camps in *Pinecrest*, clean walls which have climbing potential and adequate length are marked with a light-blue star on the topographic map in the back of this guide, and are mentioned in the description of the route that passes nearby.

Climbing near Kibbie Lake

Bibliography

Bailey, Edgar H. (ed.), *Geology of Northern California*. San Francisco: California Division of Mines and Geology, 1966

Basey, Harold E., *Sierra Nevada Amphibians*. Three Rivers: Sequoia Natural History Association, 1969

Baxter, Don J., *Gateways to California*. San Francisco: PG&E, 1968

Barrett, S. A., and E. W. Gifford, *Miwok Material Culture*. Yosemite: Yosemite Natural History Association, 1933

Buckbee, Edna Bryan, *The Saga of Old Tuolumne*. New York: The Press of the Pioneers, 1935

California Dept. of Fish and Game, *Angler's Guide to the Waters of the Emigrant Basin Area*. Sacramento: DF&G, 1964

Chisum, Gary Lee, *Ethnography of the Sierra Miwok*. Sonora: *The Quarterly of the Tuolumne County Historical Society*, 1967

Curtiss, Garness H., "Mode of Origin of Pyroclastic Debris in the Mehrten Formulation of the Sierra Nevada," in *University of Calif. pubs. in Geol. Sciences*. Berkeley: UC Berkeley, 1954

Hill, Mary, *Geology of the Sierra Nevada*. Berkeley: UC Press, 1975

Hood, Mary and Bill, *Yosemite Wildflowers and Their Stories*. Yosemite: Flying Spur Press, 1969

Hoover, M. B. *et al. Historic Spots in California*. Stanford, Stanford University Press, 1966

Ingeles, Lloyd Glenn, *Mammals of California*. Stanford: Stanford University Press, 1947

Koenig, James B., *Geologic Map of California, Walker Lake Sheet*. San Francisco: California Division of Mines and Geology, 1963

McDonnell, Lawrence R. (ed.), *Rivers of California.* San Francisco: PG&E, 1962

Niehaus, Theodore F., *Sierra Wildflowers.* Berkeley: UC Press, 1974

Peterson, Roger Tory, *A Field Guide to Western Birds.* Boston: Houghton Mifflin Company, 1941

Storer, Tracy I., and Robert L. Usinger, *Sierra Nevada Natural History.* Berkeley: UC Press, 1970

Tooker, E. W., H. T. Morris and Paul V. Fillo, *Mineral Resources of the Emigrant Basin Primitive Area, California.* Washington: US Government Printing Office, 1970

Tuolumne County Fish and Game Association, "Annual Report, Board of Directors." Sonora, 1934

Wahrhaftig, Clyde W., Course Syllabus "High Sierra — Emigrant Basin." Berkeley: U.C. Geology Department, no date

Climbing wall at 5200' in Cherry Creek Canyon

Index

Banana Lake 93
Bear Lake 48, 91
Bell Creek 42, 47, 54
Bell Meadow 42, 76
Big Lake 66, 69, 71, 97
Bigelow Lake 7
Bloomer Lake 89
Boundary Lake 38, 78, 80
Bourland Meadow 15
Buck Lakes 7, 47, 51, 52
Buck Meadow Creek 45, 77
Burst Rock 5, 53

Camp Bob MacBride 83, 104
Camp Lake 47, 91
Castle Rock 15, 27, 58
Catfish Lake 83, 86
Catfish Lake, North 85
Cherry Creek 7, 11, 36, 38, 44, 56, 95, 96, 99, 100
Cherry Creek, East Fork 38, 39, 40, 41, 65
Cherry Creek, North Fork 38, 46, 65, 66, 67, 72
Cherry Creek, West Fork 49, 56, 69, 100
Cherry Creek Canyon 95, 97, 99, 113
Cherry Lake 2, 33, 34, 100, 101
Chewing Gum Lake 47, 73, 74
Cooper Meadow 27, 57, 58, 59, 87, 90, 109, 111
Cow Meadow Lake 46, 65, 67
Coyote Lake 45, 102
Crabtree Camp 47, 73, 76

Deer Lake 50, 53, 57, 78
Douglas Lake 46

Eagle Creek 88
Eagle Meadow 87, 88
Eagle Pass 59, 87, 88, 90
East Flange Rock 61
Edyth Lake 80
Emigrant Lake 7
Emigrant Meadow Lake 7
Emigrant Wilderness 7, 31, 43, 47, 53, 58, 71, 110
exfoliation 12

Five-Acre Lake 72, 103

Gem Lake 45, 49
Gianelli Cabin 53
Gold Rush 4, 6, 10
Groundhog Meadow 44
Grouse Lake 43

Hay Meadow 59
Herring Creek 85
Horse and Cow Meadow 58
Huckleberry Lake 33, 41, 42, 46, 47
Hyatt Lake 70, 72, 73

Ice Age 10, 12, 14
Indians, Miwok 3, 4
Indians, Piute 3
Inferno Lakes 80

Jewelry Lake 49, 50
joints 12

Karls Lake 45, 102, 103
Kibbie Creek 63, 64
Kibbie Lake 63, 64
Kibbie Ridge 33, 34, 80, 101
Kole Lake 71, 102, 103

Lake Valley 73
Leighton, Fred 7, 71
Leighton Lake 7, 102, 103
Leopold Lake 92, 93
life zones 17, 19
Lily Creek 44, 48, 56, 91

Little Bear Lake 80
Long Lake 7, 78
Lord Meadow 38, 65, 95
Louse Canyon 69

Many Island Lake 14, 37
Mercur Peak 36
Mud Lake 42

Pine Valley 42, 76
Pinecrest Lake 2, 81, 86, 104
Pinecrest Peak 84
Pingree Lake 70
Piute Creek 44, 48
Piute Meadow 44, 48
Powell Lake 54
Pruitt Lake 39, 40

Red Can Lake 7, 102, 103
Relief Creek 61, 62
Relief Lake, North 62
Relief Lake, South 62, 111
Relief Valley, Lower 60
Relief Valley, Upper 62, 104
roche moutonee 14, 45, 81
Rosasco Lake 44, 69

Sachse Spring 36
Salt Lick Meadow 56
Sanguinetti Spring 58

Shingle Spring 35, 101
Spotted Fawn Lake 80
Spring Meadow 56
Stanislaus River, Middle Fork 6
Stanislaus River, South Fork 5, 6, 18, 20, 22, 23, 27, 55, 58, 81, 83, 104, 105, 107, 108, 109, 111, 113
Studhorse Meadow 44
Styx Pass 38, 80
Summit Creek 60
Swede's Camp 36

Three Chimneys 15, 27, 59, 111
Toejam Lake 56, 92

uranium 15

Waterhouse Lake 25, 86, 87, 107, 108
Whitesides Meadow 11, 15, 55, 56, 57, 59, 60, 62, 92
Wire Lakes 50, 57, 93, 94
Wood Lake 45, 46, 77, 102

Y Meadow Lake 55, 91
Yellowhammer Lake 7, 65, 67, 71, 72, 97
Yosemite National Park 36, 38, 63, 78, 80

Write for complete free catalog.

 Wilderness Press

2440 bancroft way • berkeley, california 94704
(415) 843-8080